IN-LAWS AND OUTLAWS

By C. Northcote Parkinson

PARKINSON'S LAW

THE EVOLUTION OF POLITICAL THOUGHT

THE LAW AND THE PROFITS

IN-LAWS AND OUTLAWS

BY C. NORTHCOTE PARKINSON

Illustrated by
ROBERT C. OSBORN

IN-LAWS

AND

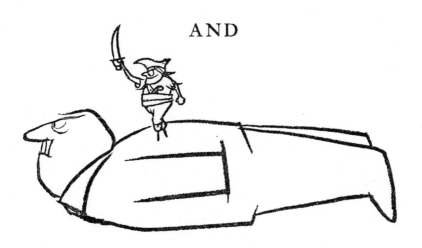

OUTLAWS

1962
THE RIVERSIDE PRESS CAMBRIDGE
HOUGHTON MIFFLIN COMPANY BOSTON

FOR ANN

PREFACE

Books on how to succeed, of which this is the latest and best, are seldom in disagreement about what success can be taken to mean. The expression "to make good," as colloquially used, may not appeal (and in fact doesn't appeal) to the philosopher or moralist, but it has at least the merit of being understood. We know, roughly, what is meant. We picture the successful man as one with high office, secure future, untarnished repute and a good press; all gained or improved by his own effort. Our mental image shows successively the house by the lake, the mature garden, the daughter's jodhpurs and the Georgian silver. With change of focus we picture the paneled office, the shining desk, the expensive tailoring and the silent car. A last angle shot reveals the exclusive club, the central figure of the central group, the modest disclaimer of sincere applause. For what? Victory, promotion, honors or another son? All four perhaps. That is what success commonly means and that is the sense in which the term will here be used.

It is not to be denied that other forms of success exist, from canonization downward. Some have given their names to exotic blooms or else dashed off immortal verse. Others have lived to an improbable age or played in concerts from the age of eight. Success can take this form or that. Granted that this is so, the reader must nevertheless expect no more than he will find. If the success in which he is interested is of the sort here first described — the sleek convertible, the private beach — this book tells all. Should he picture success in terms of reward in an afterlife or indeed of posthumous fame in this, he should seek elsewhere. No tips on martyrdom are offered between these covers. Where the word "success" is used, success in the material sense is intended. But while the success under discussion is material, it is not crude. For our present purpose, the man who makes good has not merely made money. Wealth by itself, without prestige and popularity and marred, perhaps, by parsimonious piety, is merely a form of paralysis. The art of success may involve money but must also involve sliding easily into the governing section of society, conveying the vague impression of having been there all along. In the days when motion pictures used to offer entertainment it was the custom of the impoverished to walk into the cinema backwards through the exit, saying to each other, "That was a rotten film." In much the same way the technique of success implies an unobtrusive entry into the ranks of the privileged. One must go in with all the boredom of one who is coming out. It is not enough to enter: one must also *belong*.

The advice which follows on how to succeed assumes, then, a special form of success. It also assumes that the reader is an average person but with something less than average ability. We too often see books on *How to Succeed* in which the student is urged to be more energetic, more intelligent, more helpful, more painstaking, more pleasant and more loyal than anyone else. But if he has all those merits, he has no need for the book. It is not for that sort of person that the book should be written. He will succeed anyway. The person in need of advice is *below*

average — stupid, idle, careless, uncooperative, ill-tempered
and disloyal. It is for him that books should be written.
After all, this is a democratic country. Why shouldn't he

succeed like anyone else? He can, and we shall presently
explain how. We shall assume for this purpose that success
is to be in a field of activity to which most people are assigned and for which all the others are clearly destined:
the field of public and business administration. People
imagine for themselves a career in agriculture, research,
stock-breeding, literature or field anthropology. Each sees
himself as test pilot, secret agent, ace reporter or cowboy.
All will end, if successful, at a desk; and it seems to make
little difference, in practice, whether the desk is at a university, on a rocket range, on a cattle ranch or in the
Pentagon. Come what may, that desk awaits each one of

us. We might just as well realize this from the start, beginning as we mean to continue. And once seated at a desk, our problem is how to move from desk to desk until we reach the top of the pyramid. All we need know at the outset is how to cheat in Intelligence Tests and How to dodge the Personality Screen. All this is childishly easy, the tests being designed merely to exclude (and very rightly) those who have not taken the trouble to learn how to cheat. We shall assume that these tests have been passed and that the reader already has a desk of sorts. What do you do next?

This book provides the answer. More than that, it leads you, step by step, from the most junior to the most senior positions. With this book at your bedside, success is practically unavoidable. As from this instant, your rise to power and affluence is (well, more or less) assured. But if the reader must owe so much to the author, he in turn must owe as much again to all who have helped to make this book an accomplished fact. His thanks are expressed to the editors of *The Detroit Athletic Club News, The Dude, Esquire, Fortune, Gentlemen's Quarterly, Life International, Lilliput, The New York Times Magazine*, and *Quest*, in the columns of which some of the chapters have already, in substance, appeared. He wishes also to record a debt of gratitude to Mrs. Valerie Fitchet, who typed the manuscript, to Mr. Robert C. Osborn, who did the illustrations, to Mr. Austin Olney, Miss Anne Ford and other executives, for their editorial and productive work, to the publishers themselves; and lastly to Ann, without whom the effort would have been pointless and to whom, for reasons innumerable, this book is dedicated.

C. NORTHCOTE PARKINSON

CONTENTS

IN-LAWS AND OUTLAWS

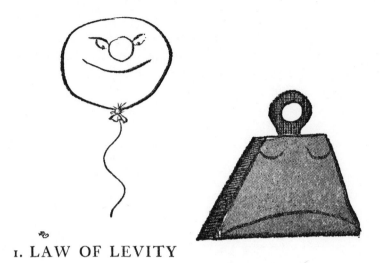

1. LAW OF LEVITY

THE AUTHOR's guidance is offered, in the first place, to the young man whose present desk is his first. It is assumed that he is in business and that his ultimate ambition is to become President of a mammoth Group of Associated Companies. But while the book's context would thus appear to be wholly industrial or commercial, the advice given is just as readily applicable to any other form of administration. One office is much like another and the principles as here laid down will apply to all. Given a desk (the basic need), with In tray, Out tray and, Pending, telephone, blotter and memo pad, the technique of success will always be the same. Your task is to find and conserve the law of Levity, the law by which the suitably gifted (or guided) individual will rise to the top of the organization chart. Contrasted with this law is that of Gravity, which holds other people down.

With one foot on the lowest rung of the ladder, your first problem will be to reconcile two quite contrasted policies. On the one hand you must hint at a more than respectable background. On the other, you must avoid spending a cent more than is unavoidable. Don't marry to begin with and don't have an apartment. Each evening, as your colleagues leave, they will see your office light still on. Each morning when they arrive they will find you already there. "How he *works!*" they will say to each other. "He practically *lives* at the office!" They will be right. That is where you will sleep. You will belong to a club for use at weekends, and on public holidays you will spend the night at a Turkish bath. Your meals at the drugstore will cost about sixty-nine cents each. Save and invest every other cent you receive. As regards your background, that should be built up on vacation.

For the first five years of your career you should spend the annual two-week vacation as follows: the first two near Groton, Exeter or Andover, the last three near Princeton, Harvard or Yale. Study the current faculty or class lists, commencement addresses and football results. Collect copies of the student newspapers. Get to know the janitors, groundsmen and police. Read all the available books and memorize all discoverable maps. Take with you, on one or two of the visits, some ambitious friend who has changed his name to Vanderbilt or Lowell. Then begin, very lightly, to touch in the background with snapshot and indirect reference. You are a graduate of Whatsitville Tech and Wheresit University, and proud of it; but these are circumstances which you need not, for the present, seek to emphasize. On no account must you tell a lie. Nothing could be more wicked, or indeed more foolish. You should

aim rather to build up *atmosphere*. When you say: "I did no rowing at Harvard—I guess I worked too hard," you will be telling the truth. When you refer to your friend Archie Lowell, and add, "We were at Groton together," you will be strictly accurate. There is no need, however, to be so specific. When some pastime like archery is mentioned, you can admit ignorance: "It was not known, I think, at Yale." Nor need you have met the film star, for "he wasn't at Princeton, was he?" In all indirect suggestion the main rule to follow is this: make up your mind which school it is to be. It is fatal to mix them. You may object that the office building contains somewhere an I.B.M. card punched full of holes, accurately recording your Whatsitville and Wheresit career, with its consistent D grades go-

ing back to kindergarten. Don't give it a thought. The office has to have these things as a symbol of status, but no one looks at record cards or does anything but file them. Without making any actual claim, without telling a single lie, without being anything but your modest self, you should become, in five years, that Ivy League man in the Public Relations Department who works harder than anyone else in the organization.

Background can be lightly indicated but money should be at least partly real. The man who saves his salary will have something to invest; hardly worth investing but useful in conversation. While playing the market cautiously and on the best advice, you should refer, very occasionally, to your large-scale operations, hinting alternatively at spectacular profit and disastrous loss. The gains and reverses will be real, representing your actual speculations but in sums greatly exaggerated. About once a year you should celebrate your gains by having five of your most talkative colleagues to an incredibly lavish dinner. Remember, however, that a loss is just as impressive. For raising of status, it is the *scale* that matters; whether the total is plus or minus is immaterial. Claim no particular prescience but confess, if you will, to having some luck. The immediate object is not, however, to suggest wealth but to claim kinship with the Rockefellers and Rothschilds. They have their market dealings and you have yours. It may thus become known that you are interested in Polychrome Plastics. "Not a *controlling* interest?" some awestruck acquaintance will ask. "Hardly that!" you will reply with a laugh, leaving him to reflect that even 43 per cent (say) of the equity would represent quite a sum.

After five years of saving and investing you should have

a capital sum at your disposal. There are various possibilities but your best plan is probably to spend it on travel. There is something to be said for quitting business for six months and reappearing with the reputation of one who knows the world. For this purpose you can rule out Europe as too well known. Something might be made of having been to Zagreb, Skopje or Santorin but their prestige value is scarcely worth the effort. Chatter about Cagliari is waste of time. The modern traveler can impress only by casual reference to Faizbad, Kaohsiung or Bandjermasin. "That reminds me," you want to be able to say, "of something that happened to me once at Ayuthia . . ." It may occur to you at this point that the Organization Man, as now conceived, needs no knowledge of the world and would be hampered, perhaps, by knowledge of any kind. This may be the approximate truth, but times are changing and you must anticipate what the change is to be. The present fashion for conformity will pass and the demand for individuality will follow. To be outstanding as an executive may be difficult but to have visited Indonesian Borneo is comparatively easy. Do something like that and so establish for good your identity as an individual; as the man who has visited Tasmania; as the man who knows the world.

Having decided upon this policy you have three alternatives between which to choose. You can visit some territory thought to be unexplored. You can learn some language known to scarcely anyone else. You can, finally, visit some scene of minor conflict and return as a military expert — or with the name of one whose past has included some reckless adventure. The main result of your travels will be a book and it is well for you to decide in advance

what the book is to be about. To travel first and then consider your impressions afterwards is unscientific and leads
to the accumulation of time-wasting and irrelevant experience. Study the bookstores and note what is being published. There are fashions, you will observe, in adventure.
But there are also good reasons for concluding that the
market is, in some directions, overstocked. No one will
now approach his publisher with a story of a child brought
up among a tribe of apes. We realize that this has been
done. Nothing is now to be gained by crossing the Pacific
on a balsa raft. Little fame will be derived from a knowledge of the Lin Yutang dialect. Least of all will service in
the Foreign Legion (should it still exist) justify another
book about adventure in Peacywrenia.

With certain avenues definitely closed, you would do
well to test your own prose style before booking your
passage.

> The canoe upsetting meant that all our supplies had been
> lost, with no stores nearer than Madlyrash, our last link
> with civilization. The journey back would take at least
> sixteen days by the river and longer by the other route.
> The rains, remember, would come in three weeks' time
> . . . I decided to push on.

The technique lies in introducing the ellipse dots at the
right point. If at all uncertain about this, decide against the
exploration business and emphasize rather your acquaintance with obscure languages and customs.

> One of the strangest characters in the vicinity was Sheer-
> ing Venshyan the peddler from Mehkbeheliv. I saw at once
> from the style of his turban that he came from the other

side of the hills and addressed him in what I hoped was the right dialect.

"Wudyanho?" I began but he merely shook his head.

"Comongsaarva?" I tried again and with a similar result. But then he solved the problem for me by muttering "Hoosyersen?" I knew then that he came, at least originally, from the north . . .

Provided you can write this sort of thing, your reputation as a linguist will be established. If you are haunted, however, as some writers are, by the fear that you will meet someone who really speaks the dialect you have pretended to master, your better plan will be to concentrate on the third or military approach. This can be attempted at two levels, the elementary and the advanced. The elementary reads rather like this:

All was silent save for the sound of machine-gun fire from the other side of the Sierra. Miguel and I approached the ruined hacienda on tiptoe, looking carefully to right

and left. Suddenly Miguel stopped and examined the
ground. I kept guard while he did so. Slowly rising to
his feet, he whispered, "Señor, eleven men passed this way
within the last half hour. I think the hacienda will be occupied." As he said this I heard a faint click as his safety
catch was released. Our eyes met for a moment—perhaps,
as we knew, for the last time. With eleven of them
against two of us, we should need to shoot straight.
"Vamos!" I whispered and our advance began . . .

This school of authorship dates from the Spanish Civil
War and has been the basis for many a reputation, being
readily transferable to South or Central America.

Military writing at the advanced level was the invention
of the late Mr. Hilaire Belloc, who did his service as a peacetime conscript in the French artillery. This made him an expert on strategy, which he still remained even after two
world wars had added something to our experience of warfare and little to our veneration for France. It is unlikely
that any modern youngster will rival Belloc as a master of
English prose but he can be readily imitated as a strategist.

The problem was essentially one of supply. With his
railhead at Pnom Penn and the road under shellfire beyond Kompong Thom, General Aix-les-Bains had to move
his infantry in at least brigade strength up to the line of
the Lam Nam. Unless this were done in six days the post
at Cheon Ksan would fall. Now, the distance from Pnom
Penn to the Lam Nam is 218 kilometers by the main road.
With his advanced troops already at Ph Rovieng it was
arithmetically just possible — but only just — for the relief column to arrive in time. The movement began on
March 14th and was unopposed until the evening of the
17th, when, at Tamesch . . . etc.

Supposing you have decided to become an explorer, the first thing is to decide on a dust jacket for the book you mean to write. Exploration dust jackets are of two kinds: those with bare bosoms and those without. They are designed for different markets, the second type of jacket sometimes taking the form of a map or the silhouette of a mountain range. On an average the first type is better business, provided the girls are reasonably attractive. Selection of such a dust cover will then narrow down your field of choice among places waiting to be explored.

These preliminaries settled, the next thing is to define the territory you mean to visit. Once again, it is a mistake to be influenced too much by the character of the country. The better policy is to write your story in outline and then find a tract of scenery which will do as background. Basically, your need is for a photogenic tributary with rapids, waterfalls and at least one crocodile. Distant mountains are an advantage and a native village for the foreground. Make an early decision as to whether there should or should not be tigers. As you are not a big-game hunter, you can well do without them. If, however, you think one essential, a good plan is to purchase some still photographs at the Zoo and superimpose them on the negative of a photograph taken locally. Some explorers take a stuffed tiger's paw with them for making tracks in the mud. This is a perfectly sound scheme, for only a trained zoologist will notice that your tracks are all made with the near hind paw: and no zoologist is likely to read your sort of book.

In writing a travel book the thing to avoid is monotony. The only remedy for this is to give your story a climax. In a tale of mountaineering the crisis comes with the conquest of Mount Wothavyu, the cairn built, the flag set up on the summit, the Sherpas buried and the peak evacuated. This happens two-thirds way through the book, leaving the last chapters for a somewhat partisan assessment of what the achievement means. At least one chapter should explain why the previous expedition failed, through having the wrong climbers, the wrong equipment, the wrong maps and the wrong food — apart altogether from their error in approaching from the wrong direction at the wrong time of the year. But mountains should play only a minor part in the sort of travel book we are discussing. Climbing feats should not be emphasized unless you are an actual climber, which we can assume you are not. It is best to throw in an oblique reference, a faked camera study and a modest disclaimer, passing on quickly to something else. So the climax of your book will not be on a virgin summit or even down an unexpected crevasse. What is the crisis to be? Of the various climaxes, the Fire in the Longhouse is probably

the best. It has served many a script writer at a loss how to finish the story and will serve many script writers in years to come. It lacks any touch of originality but it is dramatic, final and neat. It lends itself to vivid description. It disposes of unwanted characters, including The Chief's Daughter (if there has to be one). It can wipe out the whole community if you like, making your anthropological notes impossible to refute. It allows you to rescue someone — the faithful tracker, perhaps, who had never left your side in times of danger — and it rounds off the narrative in such a way as to explain why your exploring days are over.

As I looked back from the ridge towards where the last wisps of smoke were still visible among the treetops, I knew that I should never return. Why should I? It would not be the same. The happy community I had known would no longer exist. As for Hocusp Ozchus the Medicine Man, I should never know now the truth of the legend. Could he really raise people from the dead? Who can say? He certainly could not raise himself. But that he had exceptional gifts I am full convinced. Whatever his secrets may have been, they died with him. While I am no believer in the occult, I must admit that things I have seen admit of no ordinary explanation. There let the matter rest. Turning northward again, I began the long descent . . . etc., etc.

If the dramatic climax is useful in a book of exploration, it is vital to a book designed to establish the author's reputation as a linguist. The wise author will therefore build this type of book round a central and predictable event. Ideal for this purpose is the coronation of some hitherto unpublicized king. It is best to attend ceremonies of this kind in a journalistic capacity. There is no need to represent the *New York Herald Tribune*, nor yet the *Daily Telegraph*. You can go as correspondent for the *Mudborough Chronicle* or the *Poultry Fancier's Gazette*. Journals of this character will usually accept the services of anyone willing to go to Ethiopia or Nepal at his own expense. All you need from the bewildered editor is a letter stating that you are *Girls' Own* special correspondent assigned to cover the coronation at Lhasa or Bangkok. That letter is all you need to secure full journalistic privileges — which usually means sharing a bedroom with at least three other reporters, two from Patagonia and one from Taiwan.

It is the international character of the affair which will afford you the chance to show your linguistic skill. This is best done in a series of modest disclaimers. "The fact is that I know very little Serbo-Croat . . ." or, "I can understand Arabic but speak only enough for purposes of travel. The Sheikh made it clear, however, that he belonged to one of the stricter sects . . ." etc. "Any smattering I may have of Urdu was severely tested that day." The technique is to follow up a frank confession of ignorance by a scene from which your conversational fluency can be readily inferred. Your subsequent candor will then be disbelieved so that further inaccuracy may scarcely be needed. When you come to write your book, however, it is unnecessary to state that you were the special representative of the *Table Tennis Review* appointed on the grounds that table tennis is believed by the editor, on your evidence, to be the Dalai Lama's favorite recreation. You need refer only to "the famous journal of which I was at that time the correspondent," throwing in one or two references to the

1500-word cables you sent off in the small hours as the minimum coverage your news editor would expect. Remember to record your difficulty in rendering the exact meaning of the phrases used. "This prayer," you will remark, "means literally 'Hail precious stone in the brightly petaled flower' — but the expression (with its finer shades of meaning) is not really translatable." That will be enough in itself to establish your reputation as an orientalist. Leave it at that and pass on quickly to comment on the cut-glass chandeliers which the Nepalese import from the West and upon which they base their notions of prestige. Always bear your scholarship lightly, as a foible of which you are half ashamed.

Come now to the third approach, the theater of war. There is usually some minor conflict in progress at any given time and indeed there are often several, giving you two or three campaigns from which to choose. In making

your decision you must again be guided by the character of
the book you mean to write. If you are to attempt something on the advanced or Bellocian level, you must find
some campaign with a tangible enemy; one in a position to
fire back. There might seem to be an undesirable element
of danger in this but you must remember that the grand
strategist has no occasion to come within range or even earshot of the enemy guns. All he needs is a map, an almanac,
a railway timetable, a pair of dividers and a bottle of
cognac. It must, however, be admitted that wars fought
on this scale — large enough to involve strategy but not so
large as to cause real inconvenience — are infrequent. You
may be forced to take your warfare at the lower level.
That is, frankly, less attractive. Even if the other side is in
no position to shoot at you, there will be no avoiding a
measure of discomfort. You must be far enough forward
to collect your descriptive material, whether it is to be
desert or jungle. Given the background, however, the rest
is simple. You have only to listen to all the current stories
and retell them in an improved form with yourself as the
chief character. Everything you hear of as happening will
have happened to you. It is the method used by Mendez
Pinto and many another storyteller. There is every sort
of classical precedent for the technique you will use and
the result will be a very fair description of the war; omitting only the monotony of it, for that is unmarketable.
Here, as in other possible travel books, the best plan is to
rough out the story in advance. The climax will be the
ambush in which the enemy chief dies, riddled with bullets
but defiant to the end. You will be there as a war correspondent — representing, possibly, the *Elks Magazine* or
Sunday-School World — and the reader will be led to

suspect that you were leading the patrol in all but name. "No, Lieutenant," you will be thought to have said. "You should head more to the southeast, and meet the track *here*, just below the spot height 237. I *think* you should have a target at about 1500 hours — perhaps I should say 1445 hours — at 250 yards range. But don't open fire until the *third* man comes into view." All this should be obvious from the modest way in which you insist on the subaltern being given all the credit.

Half the value of your reputation will lie in your refusal to discuss these past adventures. You must become adept at reticence. "Do I speak Swahili?" You will murmur, "Good heavens, no! I have forgotten anything I ever knew. The language I should *like* to know well is Spanish — perhaps I should say Castilian. I expect you know that language, sir?" Or someone else introduces you as "the explorer." "Don't listen to him!" you implore. "You might think I had been to the Antarctic! Have you read Dog-sleigh's book on the South Pole? There is real exploration for you!" Or, finally, some hostess begs you to tell her friends about your adventures. "But, really, I have never seen a shot fired. All that stuff I wrote is just too incredibly bogus." For once in a way you will be telling the truth. Rest assured, however, that no one will believe a word of it.

2. IN-LAWS
AND OUTLAWS

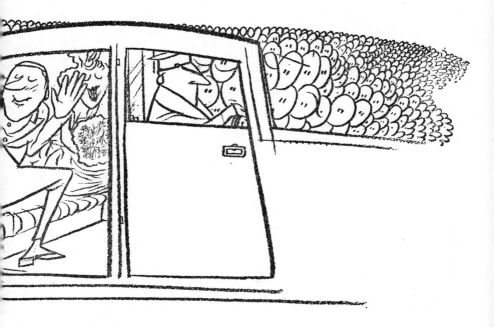

To HAVE the right background, at least by repute, and to have in addition a name for travel, knowledge and adventure (whether earned or skillfully assumed) is to gain, at the outset, a considerable advantage. Your more humdrum competitors must seem colorless by comparison and barely distinguishable from each other. Still more vital, however, is the next step in your career. Your main difficulty, as you will by now have discovered, is not in forming the right judgment but in reaching a first position in which judgment is required. There are several ways in which this can be done, one being to model yourself on men who have succeeded, another being to take a correspondence course

in leadership. But the best method of all is actually the simplest. It consists in marrying the right girl.

How is this done? You must study, first of all, the photographs taken at Society Weddings. From many of these it will be apparent that the bridegroom is judged to

be a rising man. That is obviously the category in which
you mean to be included. To assume this role you must lay
your plans with considerable care. You will realize, to begin with, that not every society wedding is relevant.
Where the marriage is between a Rothschild and a Du Pont

you will conclude that your own marriage will have to be different. The magazine illustration you should study will have a caption somewhat as follows:

> Mr. Upton Cumming with his bride, Miss Sheila Swellyn, after their marriage on May 14th at St. Stephen's Episcopal Cathedral. The bride was given away by her father, Mr. Hiram Swellyn, and the ceremony was performed by the Bishop of Vermont. The bridesmaids were the bride's cousins, Miss Prudence de Benture and Miss Verity Hardcash. Mr. Goodstock acted as best man and the guests included Mr. and Mrs. Van Wallstreet, Mr. and Mrs. Uppercrust, . . . etc. etc.

Study this picture with reverent care and you will conclude (correctly) that the bride's father is the central figure, Mr. Upton Cumming being essentially his son-in-law. Give the matter some further thought and you will come to realize that High Society is largely composed of Sons-in-Law; a fact which has only recently been established and one of which only a few are as yet aware. The fact to grasp is that your father was given you and there is little you can do about it, but your father-in-law you can choose. More than that, it is upon the choice of a father-in-law that your future career may depend. Instead of making a hasty selection among the vice-presidents of the organization in which you are or can pretend to be a key man, you should scan the market as a whole. Ascertain what fathers-in-law there may be available. To list the sources of information which should be consulted, to analyze their authenticity, to arrive at a reasonably accurate process of assessment and to define the principles upon which a selection should be made — all this would be material enough for a Ph.D. thesis. There is no space here for such an exhaustive study. All that can be done is to dispel one common illusion and suggest a few basic rules.

The illusion concerns the possibility of marrying an heiress. Behind this is the theory that men of ability tend to produce more daughters than sons. For this theory (ex-

cept, possibly, as applied to university professors) the evidence is insufficient. There is evidence, moreover, which actually points in the other direction. A recent survey of a hundred successful men showed that twenty-three are childless; and not unreasonably so in the case of those who never married. The remainder had, it was found, some 215 children between them, 112 male and 103 female. Numbers

in the family ranged, it was noted, from one to eight, the commonest totals being two or three. What is depressing, from the bachelor's angle, is that only thirteen of these wealthy men have daughters only, and of these only five have restricted their offspring to one. With only five definite sole heiresses, and eight more with younger sisters to consider, the field is not and has never been extensive. And even from this discouragingly low total we must make

deductions in respect of those over fifty years of age, those
who turn out to be bankrupt and those — probably the
remainder — who are already married. It would be rash
to generalize on the basis of these figures, but further research would probably justify our tentative conclusion that
the chances of inheriting vast fortunes by marriage are
relatively low. The sons are far too numerous and the only
daughters are far too few. These are the sad facts and there
is no escaping them.

Even with an unmarried heiress in sight, the predatory
bachelor might well hesitate. For marrying money can
easily involve the extinction of your family. The girl with
no brothers may come of stock with a female strain and so
breed only daughters in her turn. If her brothers were
killed, that admittedly alters the picture, but there should
be some careful investigation of the circumstances which
have left her the heiress. In times past, the traditional alternative before the young nobleman was to marry money, as
his parents advised, or to marry a chorus girl, as he himself
might prefer. It was the latter course which often proved
the wiser, at least genetically. Only quite recently has it
been possible to marry a chorus girl with money; and then
the marriage seems to last only two years. For various

reasons, therefore, the plan for marrying wealth should be abandoned. Failure in such a scheme would be more than likely and success might be fatal.

While it may not be practicable to gain wealth by marriage it *is* possible to marry into a family with influence. More than that, it is constantly being done. Turn the pages of the illustrated magazine and you will find a group picture of the distinguished people now staying with Mr. Vanderfeller at his ranch near Carmel. There is Senator Dimwit, Gloria Stormsign (film star), the Duke of Spumante, Oscar Hardcover (novelist) and Olga Volga (television). The group also includes two young men, Mark Smith and Alec Brown, seen talking to the Vanderfellers' daughters. But why these two in particular? Why not Robinson, Baker or Jones? What have these two that others lack? To this question there is no obvious answer but the fact of their presence everywhere is undeniable. They are clearly potential sons-in-law, the Men of Promise. The urgent question is how to become one of them.

In approaching this difficult problem the axiom to observe is that you need not try to impress everybody. There are people who do it but it leaves them no leisure for anything else. Your best plan is to choose your father-in-law and begin your campaign from there. Instead of aiming at universal popularity you have merely to gain the good opinion of one important man. Who is it to be? The choice would be simpler if the possible names had been collected in a single work of reference, but nothing of the sort has ever been done. You will have realized without prompting that your list of possible fathers-in-law must be confined to men *who have daughters.* Many a young man has sought to ingratiate himself with a wealthy newspaper proprietor or brewer only to find that he is childless or the father, merely, of innumerable sons. All this stems from sheer carelessness and deserves no sympathy. The man whose respect you seek to gain must be influential, wealthy and the father of at least one daughter. One with several daughters is, of course, preferable, your chances being thereby multiplied.

Let us suppose that your short list, when drawn up, comprises the junior Senator for the state of Omega, the Governor of Disconnecticut, the President of U.S. Pig Iron, the Sultan of Gushing-Arabia, the recent Ambassador to Myopia and the chief proprietor of *Tide*. Let us suppose that a careful comparison of their claims narrows the first choice down to one. Mr. Miles Leeding, president of U.S. Pig Iron, is, for some reason or another, the man you think most suitable. As is well known he has (in addition to two sons) no less than three unmarried daughters; Angela, Barbara and Caroline, born in alphabetical order and aged respectively twenty-six, twenty-three and nineteen. Their father owns not only half of U.S. Pig Iron but a controlling interest in Blackgold Oilfields, Inc., of Texas and extensive interests in the Argentine, Canada, Nicaragua and Panama. The family seems to be influential as well as prosperous. Which daughter is it to be? The deciding factor is age. A wife should on marriage be half her husband's age plus seven years. If you are twenty-four you should try to secure Caroline; if thirty-one, Barbara and if thirty-six, Angela. Should you be, say, twenty-nine, Caroline might be the first choice with Barbara in reserve.

This policy decided upon, it remains only to make yourself known to Mr. and Mrs. Leeding; and that, for the unenterprising, is the main obstacle. It need not be insurmountable by those who have studied this chapter with the rapt attention it deserves. A writer on modern warfare used to write frequently about the Strategy of Indirect Approach. Whether that is a good idea in warfare may be a matter for dispute but the principle is certainly applicable to the problem we are studying. To rush at Mr. Leeding and say "I want to marry one of your daughters" would be a tactical error. The occasion is one for stratagem, subtlety and finesse. And the essence of the technique is to begin, as in any scientific enterprise, with RESEARCH.

Begin by listing and making full notes on the Leedings' nearest relatives; their names and whereabouts; their special interests; and whether they are on speaking terms with the family concerned. If you refer to Mr. Miles Leeding, for research purposes, as A and his wife as B, your card index entries might read like this:

Se-rial	Name	Family Re-lationship	Real Re-lationship	Special Interests
1.	Mr. Form-leigh Leeding	A's elder brother	Mutual loathing	Bank President Breeds mink
2.	Mr. Hardley Leeding	A's younger brother	Mildly friendly with A	Master of the Hark Forrard Hunt, North Carolina
3.	Mr. Nevil Leeding	A's youngest brother	Intimate with A	Collects and writes about old dueling pistols
4.	Miss Leeding	A's only sister	Neutral	Vice-president of the Society for the Pre-vention of practically everything
5.	Mrs. Barbara Bloodworthy	Elder sis-ter of B. Married to No. 6	Intimate with B	Strong supporter of Confederate Cause and admirer of Gen. Lee
6.	General Mark Bloodworthy	Brother-in-Law of B. Married to No. 5.	Friendly with A	Hunting, tuna fishing, describing how he won World War II
7.	Miss Ailsa McGaelic	Younger sister of B. Unmarried	Hostile to everyone Detested by A	Practices Yoga & Zhen Buddhism. Has visited Tibet. Tries to convert B to her views
8.	Miss Agatha Bloodworthy	Sister of No. 6	Friendly with B	An ardent feminist. Principal of St. Ursula's Liberal Arts College

There might well be more than eight entries in such a list as this, many of them (like No. 4) of negligible value. But these few are enough to illustrate the principles by which you should be guided. First, decide which is the more formidable, A or B. Should it be A, the possibilities between which you have to choose are these:

1. You can write an article to prove that the breeding of mink is a vice beside which the crimes of Nero fade into insignificance.
2. You can find an unusual pair of dueling pistols and ask No. 3 to identify them.
3. You can join the Friends of the Confederate Cause and ingratiate yourself with No. 5.
4. You can write to No. 6 and ask his opinion as to how World War II was won.
5. You can allege that No. 7 has never been to Tibet, or
6. You can lecture at St. Ursula's College in such a way as to prove the superiority of women.

You can, for that matter, try all these approaches simultaneously. The most effective way would be to lecture at St. Ursula's College on Old Firearms, ensuring that Nos. 2, 5, 6 and 7 are present, with 8 of course presiding. Use the rare dueling pistols to illustrate the lecture, with a live mink as the target. Kill the mink with the first shot and wound Aunt Ailsa accidentally with the second. End the lecture by pointing out that Confederate Generals never bred Mink, judging (as they did) that their wives would do it better; that World War II was nearly lost by male mink breeders but won at the eleventh hour by men with a real knowledge of tuna fishing and hunting. If you are not invited to the Leeding Ranch after that, the family is clearly not worth bothering about. The chances are, however, that you will find yourself an honored guest within a matter of weeks, Caroline being told to marry you whether she wants to or not. Should there be any sales resistance on her part you can possibly secure the eldest by pretending an interest in the next. The engagement announced, you will

shortly enter the select market of the world's Sons-in-Law.

If all goes well, the first symbol of your success will be the publication of a group photograph: "Mr. and Mrs. Miles Leeding with their guests at Buenavista, their summer home near Monterey," with you shown as one of the younger people clustered round the swimming pool. Next will come the portrait of Miss Angela Leeding, whose engagement has just been announced. The same periodical will also publish a charming view of San Rafael Island in the West Indies, vacation residence of her fiancé, Mr. Aubrey Reeder. Does such a place exist? Almost certainly, one would imagine, but there is no need for you to own it. An island is easily borrowed and a picture of one more easily still. Last of all comes the wedding group outside the Episcopal Cathedral. As from that moment you will be definitely *in*. Why? Because your wife's relatives cannot afford to have failures in the family. Their affection for you may be strictly limited. Their affection for her may tend to diminish. But their own credit is involved, to some extent, in your success. For just as you will refer to them, casually, as relatives, so they cannot avoid referring (less frequently) to you. "The Supernational Banking Corporation?" You will say, "Of course I know it. My wife's uncle is the President." "North Carolina? No, I have never been there. My uncle by marriage keeps a pack of hounds there, however, and I'm looking forward to our first visit." "Big-game fishing? I never had the time until last year, when Mark Bloodworthy took me out in his cruiser *Snapdragon*. Boy, was that exciting!" To be able to make these references may gain you nothing more than prestige. But what when business acquaintances ask Mr.

Miles Leeding about Angela? "Shall we be seeing your married daughter at Palm Beach?" and "How's your son-in-law doing, Miles?" and "I hear, Miles, that you have a grandson. Congratulations!" For the sake of his own status, your father-in-law cannot afford to have you anything less than Vice-president. With whatever misgivings, he will have to see that you are promoted.

You are now one of the world's In-Laws. But what would your fate have been had it happened otherwise? You would have been a No-Law or an Outlaw, and these are terms which we must now define. A No-Law is an eligible

bachelor, one who must make his way unaided but about whom there lingers the romance of one still available. There are minor advantages in this role, provided you are not too low in the Corporation's hierarchy. The typists will work for you more willingly and the mothers of the less attractive girls will ask you to parties. Rumors may circulate about your broken heart, about the heiress to whom you were engaged but who died of diphtheria, about the starlet who finally married someone else, about the French Countess whose family forbade the match on religious grounds, about the Austrian Princess who entered a convent so as to avoid being married to your rival. Such rumors will go around, provided you originate them, and will do you no harm. Neither, however, can they do you much good. As compared with an In-Law the No-Law is in a weak position, any hint of mystery about his past being as likely to repel as attract. Minor advantages apart, his main asset lies in the fact that he may still become an In-Law. As compared with the Outlaw, the No-Law is at least a Man of Promise. His cards are still to play.

Hard is the lot, by contrast, of the Outlaw. His mistake has been to marry the wrong girl. This comes about, normally, through marrying at too early an age. He never forgot that blonde he knew at High School. He remained loyal to the brunette he loved at College. He fell for the redhead who typed his first letters as a young executive. Whichever it is, he has tied himself by marriage to the environment from which he is trying to escape. The High School blonde is attractive only by the standards of Flatville, which are of course appallingly low. The College brunette may have been the best of the bunch at Whatsitville Tech — but what a dreary bunch that must have been! As for the office redhead she is merely the smartest girl of the five who are still unmarried. It is the itch to marry the girl next door which is the mark of those predestined for merely average success. For while such a wife may be anxious, in general, for you to succeed, she will not want your success to go beyond a certain point. She will retain her small-town outlook. In a larger circle of more prosperous friends she would find herself below the average in looks, family, brains and knowledge. Her unspoken preference is for a society in which she can be well above the average. Down to that level she will try to keep you and the odds are that she will succeed. It is thus usually fatal to marry the girl next door.

To this rule there is one significant exception. A woman sufficiently beautiful can make her way at any level of society. Married to a girl of stunning appearance a man may have his moments of anxiety but he will not, in general, find that she hinders his career.

Nubility or fitness for marriage can be measured by a formula as here to be revealed for the first time. It depends upon careful investigation and survey. Where this is impossible, however, or where a snap decision is needed, the generally accepted tests can be applied in a shortened form. Look at her eyes to see what a girl was born with. Look at her hands to see what she has learned. Look at her mouth to see what she has become. There can be no pretense at accuracy in this hurried valuation but it follows the same pattern as the more careful assessment. It is obviously preferable to apply the test at leisure, aiming at a precision which we know to be finally unattainable but using nevertheless such science as we can. From the table which follows it will be evident that there are four general aspects of quality, A, B, C, and D. Each can be either positive or

negative, with values graded from A to D and (on the negative scale) from E to H. Using the methods of simple arithmetic, a man of any ambition should normally reject any idea of marrying a girl whose negative qualities outweigh the positive so that

$$E + F + G + H > A + B + C + D$$

Girls with a zero score are not and should not be in great demand.

Plus Factors		Marks		
1.	Health & Beauty	20		
2.	Vitality & Energy	10	40	A
3.	Intelligence	10		
4.	Good Family Background	20		
5.	Athletic Skill & Aptitude	5	30	B
6.	Knowledge	5		
7.	Loyalty	10		
8.	Good Disposition & Manners	5	20	C
9.	Social Ease & Popularity	5		
10.	Income & Expectations	10	10	D
			100	

Minus Factors		Marks		
1.	Poor Appearance & Health	20		
2.	Idleness & Inertia	10	40	E
3.	Stupidity	10		
4.	Unpleasant Relatives & Friends	15		
5.	Carelessness & Clumsiness	10	30	F
6.	Ignorance	5		
7.	Infidelity	10		
8.	Quarrelsomeness & Bad Manners	5	20	G
9.	Snobbishness & Unpopularity	5		
10.	Extravagance & Indebtedness	10	10	H
			100	

Girls with a positive rating will have a score from 1 to 100, obtained by simple addition, the result being the N.R. or Nubility Rating. These totals give us, in turn, the Nubility Classification (N.C.) as follows:

	Class
100 - 85	I
84 - 70	II
69 - 55	III
54 - 40	IV
39 - 25	V
24 - 10	VI

Girls with a score below 10 are unclassified.

The Male Nubility Rating is obtained by using the same table, substituting "good appearance" for "beauty" in Plus Factor 1, and "salary, status and prospects" for "income and expectations" in Plus Factor 10. A man who fails to qualify had best forget the whole idea and turn at once to the next chapter. One who classifies, however, can fairly decide how high he should aim. A Class III man could thus reasonably dream of securing a Class II girl, while a man in Class I might normally hope to marry a girl in Class I.

But the man for whom this book is written, the man who seeks to rise in the world, is rarely in Class I, having lost marks heavily in family background, knowledge, disposition, popularity and income. He is probably in Class III at best. But his policy, as we have seen, is to marry a girl with a good family background, ignoring the fact that her N.C. may be as low as IV or V. He thus becomes an In-Law. Had he, however, married the girl next door, he would probably have found himself with a wife in Class V or VI. This would automatically make him an Outlaw,

having married two or three Classes below expectations
without any compensating factor in section (4). It is not
to be denied that Outlaws occasionally succeed in life but
for this they need quite exceptional gifts. An In-Law can
succeed, by contrast, with gifts below the average and indeed with no obvious merit of any kind. It is for this reason that such emphasis is given here on the question of
marriage. For should you make an early and unsuitable
marriage or should your plans for becoming an In-Law
go astray, you will have to rely only on Yourself in what
you will find to be a highly competitive world.

3. NONORIGINATION

As a young businessman, you should learn early in life that your advice is of no value to your elders and betters. It is normally futile to approach them with a plan for reorganizing the business, for such a plan implies that it needs reorganizing — the most insulting suggestion one businessman can make to another. And even were the suggestion acceptable from anyone, it would not be acceptable from *you*. Who are *you*, a mere deputy assistant, to tell the directors how their business should be run? Submit your memorandum, expecting promotion to result, and you will find yourself before the President — but not merely to receive his congratulations.

President   Reading this memorandum, Mr. Reeder, I find myself wondering who is the chief executive here, me or you.

Reeder   You are, sir.

President   Me? But I evidently know nothing about the

business. After thirty years as a manufacturer, I still need guidance (it would seem) from the most junior people in the office. Does this strike you, Mr. Reeder, as unusual?

Reeder   Yes, sir; I mean, no sir.

President   You think, perhaps, that my methods are out of date?

Reeder   No, sir. Certainly not, sir.

President   You realize that I have had years of experience? And you realize that you have had none? But you still think that you know best?

Reeder   Yes — no — I mean yes, sir.

President   You realize that executives have been fired for making suggestions only half as insolent as these? Do you expect me to be more lenient with you?

Reeder   No, sir — yes — I mean, no sir.

President (*gently and quietly*)   Merely for your own good, Mr. Reeder, I advise you to keep your ideas to yourself until you have more experience. Try to believe that those senior to you know what they are doing. Try to recall that this business was conducted, somehow, before you were born. Try to imagine that it could go on without your help. Try to learn, reflect and consider. In the meanwhile [*suddenly screams*] GET OUT!!

This type of interview does nothing to hasten your promotion or ensure your peace of mind. It is best for that reason to approach the whole matter from a different angle. We shall suppose, for this purpose, that your scheme is perfectly sound and will save the corporation half a million each year. In putting it forward, you can have three possible objects. First, you can add to the Corporation's prosperity. Second, you can gain the reputation of being clever. Third, you can so alter the hierarchy's structure that your own position becomes more important — as, for example, in creating a new post which only you can fill. The first two of these objects you can dismiss at once. The Corporation's prosperity (unless it is actually tottering) is none of your business. A reputation for cleverness is the last thing you want, nor could it lead to anything but trouble. Only the third object could justify your taking action. And there are, even then, two major pitfalls of which you must be aware from the start. In the first place, your motive is likely to be obvious. In the second place, the new vacancy may go to someone else. You will end, if unlucky, with the reputation of an intriguer and of one whose intrigues fall completely flat. This is not the sort of reputation you wish to establish.

How often did it happen during World War II that a Lieutenant Colonel (General Staff) would produce a reorganization scheme by which a headquarters establishment came to be considerably expanded. Accepting the scheme for which he had pleaded so eloquently, the General would gaze at the new organization chart with the appreciation of a connoisseur.

"Yes, yes, yes," he would mutter as he adjusted his spectacles. "A very effective solution to our difficulties. I notice, by the way, that this establishment includes a vacancy for a Brigadier."

"The upgrading became essential," the Lieutenant Colonel would admit with a modest cough. "It followed

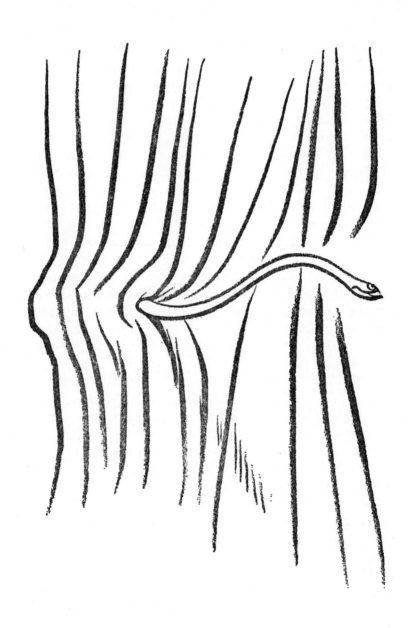

from the readjustment of duties at the Grade II level."

"Just so, just so," the General would murmur. "Upgrading becomes inevitable. I shall have to make a recommendation."

Blushing slightly and glancing downward, the Lieutenant Colonel would begin to word the letter he would be writing home. "It came," he might say, "as a complete surprise . . ."

"Yes," the General would repeat sadistically, "I shall have to make a recommendation . . . and I know the very man. Brigadier Coldsteel of the First Parachute Division, one of my oldest friends. He comes out of hospital next week. The very man!" (*Telephones*) "Get me the base hospital. . . . All right, I'll hold on. . . ." Turning once more to the Lieutenant Colonel, he would add, brightly, "And now I have *another* problem. What am I to do with *you?*"

This is not the sort of situation in which you should place yourself. It is essential, therefore, that any scheme you originate should be put forward by someone else who honestly believes that the idea was his in the first place. Neither praise nor blame need come your way, nor can it be thought that you stooped to intrigue. Of all the administrative techniques there is none, probably, of more importance than the art of having your views put forward by someone else. Towards this desirable result the first step is to choose your stalking horse. It must be somebody to whom the President will listen, somebody fairly senior, somebody who is open to suggestion and somebody without too many ideas of his own. There is such a man in every organization and we shall call him Harry Bumbling. He is a keen member of the Country Club and it is there

that you will push your acquaintance. Your attitude from
the start must be one of humble admiration. "I wish I had
your knowledge of the business," you will sigh. "It must
take years of experience to develop your sureness of judgment!" "How strange," you will protest, "that a man of
your seniority should retain so youthful and fresh an outlook!" Before long you will be able to insist on his daring
and original ideas. "There is no one but you who could
have thought of that, Harry. We all know by now where
the President gets his ideas!"

Having established a relationship as of master and dis-
ciple you wait for the next occasion of festivity and waylay
Harry Bumbling in the Men's Toilet. You need to be
rather more sober than he is.

"Say, Harry, this scheme of yours for making K Division
a separate company — I think that's a wonderful idea!"

"What scheme?"

"Brent has just told me about it. In strict confidence,
mind you. And do you know what I said?"

"How could I? I wasn't there, was I?"

"Well, I said to him, 'Brent,' I said, 'that man's a genius!'
Did I mean it? I'll say I meant it."

"You meant what?"

"I meant it when I called you a genius."

"Why?"

"Because of your scheme for K Division."

"What scheme?"

"For making K Division a separate company — Brent
told me about it."

"What is Brent?"

"Brent Bablock. But I guess it's secret and he shouldn't
have told me."

"Sure it's secret. Why can't he keep his big mouth shut?"

"He sure does talk too much. But the scheme is great. The smartest idea I ever heard — from the tax angle alone — yes, Harry, a stroke of genius!"

"What is?"

"Your scheme for K Division."

"Oh, that. But keep it under your hat."

"Strictly between ourselves. Let's get us a drink."

"Good idea. A brainwave!"

"No, you're the man for the brainwaves. The rest of us are not in the running."

"Who said I was running?"

"I never said you were — Oh, never mind. Let's go and drink to your scheme."

"What scheme?"

If you handle the matter correctly, old Bumbling will emerge from the party with a vague idea of having discussed something of momentous importance with somebody. Next day he will wonder what he discussed with whom. It will be for you to remind him and preferably over the telephone. This will set the rumors going from the Head Office switchboard.

"That you, Harry? I think I should tell you there has been some leakage about your scheme for K Division — the idea we were discussing last night. Everyone is talking about it. They all think it quite brilliant."

"Brilliant? Oh, I wouldn't say that. Basically quite a simple idea."

"A simple idea which occurred to no one else! Actually it was the application of the scheme which impressed me even more. You have the thing worked out to the last detail."

"Have I? Well, I mean, it doesn't do to be vague."

"I was so impressed, Harry, that I made some notes as soon as I got home. I hope they are an accurate account of what you had in mind."

"Perhaps you had better send them over for me to check."

"I'll do that right away. Another thing though. Two difficulties occur to me. You will know the answers, I'm sure, but I feel bound to point them out. Would you be interested?"

"Yes I should. Let's meet for lunch. At twelve-thirty in the Sports Club."

"Thanks very much. That will be fine. It's very good of you to discuss Company policy with me. Junior as I am, I can contribute nothing. But I am keen to learn."

"Glad to give you any guidance I can. At twelve-thirty then. Goodbye."

The arrival of your notes, incoherent as they may be, will solve Bumbling's main problems for him. He will know what it is he is supposed to have suggested. There will be nothing particularly clever about it but nothing manifestly unreasonable. There will be several inaccuracies in your notes and he will automatically correct them. At least one word will be misspelled, over which he can smile: "These young fellows don't know everything!" He will see at a glance how things could be put into shape and paragraphed properly. Not a bad scheme, though. With each penciled correction, he will be accepting responsibility for it. With each improvement the idea will become more definitely his.

Over lunch you will raise your two objections. These must be prepared with considerable care. Although just plausible enough to arouse interest, they must admit of a quick and final answer. One could be a point in law, something about company registration in the state of Wisconsin. "But the new company," says Bumbling, "will be registered in Idaho!" "But of course!" you will exclaim. "How stupid of me to forget that!" Your second objection can be a little more difficult, something about raising the capital for expansion, investors no longer having the security offered by the organization as a whole. This will be another skittle to knock down, probably at the second shot. The object of this maneuver is to give Bumbling the sensation of victory. He has overridden two objections to his scheme. Who will oppose him next? A further object is to dispel any lurking suspicion that the whole idea is really yours. Why, the stupid young fellow was against it at first — could do nothing but think up difficulties! Very helpful since, mind you, and worked hard over the scheme in its later stages. Under good direction, might be a useful assistant manager. Not too much initiative as yet, but that may be a good fault. There is nothing more intolerable than a young man who thinks he can run the Company. Young Reeder knows his place — that is something in his favor. Originality may come with more experience. He might have a future — who knows? — as manager. Yes, a useful man.

So the originator of the scheme receives none of the applause? None at all. He must reject from the outset the least suggestion that the idea came from anyone but Bumbling. This is in accordance with a general principle of administration. Always have your ideas put forward by someone else. The man in control of the committee is often the man who says nothing. Pursue the opposite

policy, advocating a scheme and expecting to gain credit by its adoption and you may well succeed — just once. By that one success you will have created the opposition to anything else you may propose. With the reputation of being too clever by half, you will be sidetracked into work of lessening importance. Your career, at least in the organization that you first joined, will end before it has begun. Your only policy will be to start afresh, having read this book, and make a different impression on a different group of people. In the new organization to which you have transferred there may well be someone to whom the president will listen, somebody fairly senior, somebody who is open to suggestion and somebody without too many ideas of his own. He is a keen member, as it happens, of the Country Club and it is there that you will meet. Your attitude from the start will be one of humble admiration . . . You may know nothing of the business but you will know something, by now, about human nature.

4. EXPERTISE

IN THE COURSE of your business career you will hear constantly of experts in Organization and Method. You will eventually meet them and wonder, perhaps, whether this is a career which you might yourself adopt. You will have realized, after all, that doing a job is more difficult than telling someone else how the job ought to be done.

The temptation is a real one but it should be resisted. That
vocation is not for you. As against that, you will often have
to deal with Business Consultants. You do well, therefore,
to study their habits and make yourself fully acquainted
with the nature of their business. They have come to form
a permanent feature of the business landscape, prominent,
vociferous and inescapable.

But let there be no misconception about this. Nothing in
this book should be taken as a reflection on the experts in
Organization and Method. There are many consultants
whose respectability is beyond question and many others
against whom nothing has actually been proved. More
than that, the business of consultation is on the increase.
To the industrial corporation the expert in method is the
equivalent of the psychiatrist and the tranquilizer, being
called into play when the strain is proving too much for
its constitution, equilibrium and nerves. Just as the troubles
confided to the psychiatrist are lessened by being shared,
as also by the realization that they are far from unique,
so the feverish pulse of a large organization will slow down
when the business consultant appears and before he has
uttered a word of advice. "Yes, yes, yes," he will murmur
soothingly. "Lights burning late in the office, friction over
the parking facilities, ill-tempered behavior at lunch; all
the well-known symptoms — just like a case I attended last
week." But the bedside manner is not the whole of his
stock-in-trade, nor is sympathy all he has to offer. Sooner
or later he will give positive advice — and that is what
leaves us puzzled.

In a business corporation headed by a president of eminence, run by directors of experience and overflowing with
executives of proved competence and zeal, it must always

seem strange that consultants should have to be called in from outside to advise on how the work should be distributed. If the directors don't know how to organize the concern it seems fair to ask what they do know and for what, indeed, they are being paid. It is also natural to wonder what reason there can be for supposing that outside consultants should know what the Board do not. These questions, which have long baffled the public at large, would seem to deserve an answer.

We can reasonably assume, to begin with, that the consultants know very little. Their right to advise derives essentially from their initial act in putting up their shingles: "Sneering, Shockwell and Foggarty, Business Consultants," or "Sadleigh, Deep, Loring and Muddleworth, Efficiency Engineers." Everything has to have a beginning and, for the methods expert, this is it. What were Foggarty and Muddleworth doing before they proclaimed their expertise? This is by no means apparent. They may have taken a correspondence course. They may have attended a class in ethics at the Harvard School of Business Administration. They may merely have failed to earn their living in any other way. But whatever their precise experience has been, there they are, experts in expertise, self-proclaimed magicians of the business world. Hardly has their bronze tablet been screwed to the doorpost before the first corporation vice-president is hammering for admission. As the line forms in the corridor the skilled observer will note that the gathering crowd of business executives includes few, if any, representatives of the government. No General is there, pausing in the midst of a campaign and anxious for advice as to whether he should withdraw or attack. No Admiral has rushed ashore to sob his troubles into a sympathetic ear. And if the President of the United States is among these jamming the entry, we must conclude that his disguise, at least, is good.

The middle-aged men blocking the sidewalk are drawn almost solely from the world of industry and commerce. They are qualified, decisive, tough and keen. The president of the corporation which makes celluloid goldfish knows just how his product should be manufactured, advertised and sold. The managing director of the firm which produces plastic balloons knows more, it is said, about elasticity and bursting-point than anyone else in that mammoth industry. The sales manager of Lollipops, Inc., is unequaled in his grasp of stickiness, lumber, sugar content and color preference. There is no one in the crowd who does not know his business. And yet they all seek advice, as it seems, of Sadleigh, Deep, Loring and Muddleworth. Why, for heaven's sake? What does Sadleigh know about celluloid? As little as Deep knows of balloons or Loring of lollipops. What magic formula is it that these experts have to sell?

A careful survey has now established the fact that the clients who approach a business consulting firm do so with one of two motives. On the one hand, they may want scapegoats for the reorganization upon which they have already decided. On the other, they may want to prevent such a reorganization taking place. The contrast between these two procedures can best be illustrated by reference to two recent case histories. For obvious reasons the identity of both the corporations and their business consultants will be concealed under names which are purely fictitious. Of the two corporations concerned, the first we shall call Horseless Carriage Co., Inc., mass-producers of veteran cars. The second we shall call Historic Homes, Inc., mass-producers of prefabricated houses, each with a prefabricated story of how George Washington slept there and with whom.

The directors of the Horseless Carriage Company of Detroit decided recently to streamline their organization. They decided, therefore, to fire half their executives and demand some real work from the other half. Their problem was how to do this without being tarred and feathered in the middle of the company parking lot. In order to avoid this, they agreed that their proposed reorganization should be the work of outside consultants. So they called in Messrs. Sneering, Shockwell and Foggarty and explained briefly what advice they expected to receive. In such a situation as this, the consultant's chief advantage is that he need not linger on the scene. He presents his report with one foot in the jet aircraft's door, reaching 20,000 feet before anyone has finished reading the first paragraph

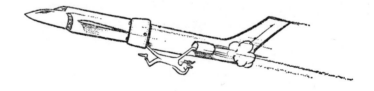

(which consists entirely of thanks to all for their cooperation). These particular consultants work as a team. Once briefed on what the policy is to be, they go swiftly into action. Sneering is condescending in a supersilly way — "Is that your *latest* I.B.M.?" "You have never heard, I suppose, of marginal costing?" and so forth. Shockwell is direct and brutal. "You carry absurdly swollen overheads." He says firmly, "You should cut down by 52 per cent." Foggarty follows up with an involved explanation of why the changes are necessary. On this occasion the results of their incursion into the business can be tabulated as follows:

(a) Half the executives were fired.
(b) A digital computer costing $1,000,000 was acquired as a symbol of progress.
(c) All partitions were demolished, making a general office out of the space previously occupied by individual offices, and
(d) The office color scheme, which had been primrose and white, was changed to lilac and gray.

Very different (at first sight) was the influence of Sadleigh, Deep, Loring and Muddleworth upon the organization of Historic Homes, Inc. The directors of Historic Homes had been under pressure from a group of stockholders whose noisy spokesmen, Barker and Maybite, insisted that the firm's organization should be modernized. What exactly they meant by this proposal was never very clear but they did not scruple to suggest that the directors were grossly overpaid considering that their responsibilities concerned only an unmodernized firm. Faced by this dangerous movement, the president called in the experts. Their instructions, on this occasion, were to report that the organization (except in one or two minor respects) was just fine the way it was. In this other group of consultants there is a different allocation of work. Sadleigh shakes his head, Deep looks profound, Loring specializes in a subtle compromise between a roar and a leer, and it is Muddleworth who enters into an obscure and involved explanation of why the changes are essential or (as in this case) needless. As a result of their incursion into the business, the following changes were made:

(a) Messrs. Barker and Maybite became directors.
(b) A digital computer costing $1,000,000 was acquired as a symbol of progress.
(c) The general office was divided up by partitions to form individual offices, and
(d) The office color scheme, which had been lilac and gray, was changed to primrose and white.

There would thus seem to be a complete contrast between the advice given in these two cases. Such a contrast there may be but the point of significance is that, on both occasions, the efficiency expert did something which the directors could not do for themselves. In the one instance they took the blame for a purge which would have been impossible for those who had to live afterwards in the same neighborhood. In the other instance their function was to assure the shareholders that the whole organization had now been modernized (whatever that means) and that there could be nothing more to worry about. As regards the partitions and paintwork it would be wrong, incidentally, to suppose that any of the experts had any strong preference either way. Their object was simply to demonstrate that something had been done.

While the two case histories just outlined are clearly typical, it would be a mistake to assume that the experts never have anything more useful to say. No one with experience in teaching could make that rash assumption, for he must instantly perceive where the consultants have another advantage. Every teacher must at some time have had the experience of being asked, at short notice, to examine in some subject of which he knew practically nothing. To the novice such an abrupt request may bring a moment of dismay. To the older teacher, it is no more than a nuisance, for he knows how the situation should be handled. When the scripts arrive he sorts out the half-dozen which appear to be legibly, neatly and competently done. Reading these, he soon discovers what the right answers are supposed to be, at least for the purposes of that particular examination. Then he marks down the others for giving answers that are different and so presumably incorrect. In the same way the efficiency engineer has opportunities for comparing one organization with another. He guesses which are the best and can then criticize the others for not being the same. In this way his advice, if it is really wanted — and it very occasionally is — can be surprisingly sensible.

Biologists tell us that trees and plants are pollinated by the bees as they pass from one to another — a process now often mechanized but still essentially the same. The efficiency expert is the bee of industry, buzzing from one industrial plant to the next and pollinating as he goes. Many a bee will stoutly maintain, no doubt, that the pollen is his own invention, perfected by a secret process unknown to the other bees. Such a bee is a liar and so, normally, is the consultant who pretends to have ideas of his own. The ideas, like the pollen, come from another plant. And the intensity of this cross-fertilization is in proportion to the

number of the bees. Bee keepers still living can recall a
period when they had to pay a rent for bee pasture. With
a fuller knowledge, it is now the orchard proprietor who
may have to pay the bee keeper for his cooperation. In
these circumstances the bee populations will increase.
Business consultants do the same, the fact that they are in
demand being proved by the fact that they are in such
large supply. And there are all sorts of situations in which,
lacking their help, a businessman could seek advice only
from his competitors. The point may have been reached,
however, when the experts have become too numerous.
That would be no proof, however, that bees are useless in
themselves. Granted that pollination may become excessive, it remains true that pollination must be done.

A problem which remains is to decide how the bee
knows a good flower from a bad. Granted that the business method consultant will carry ideas from one organization to another, how are we to know that the ideas chosen
are the best? If the examiners can find what the right
answers are from a glance at the handwriting, by what
similar method can the efficiency expert choose any one
organization as a model for the others? And our anxiety

on this score is intensified by our knowledge of what happens in school administration. It is a known fact that school inspectors, buzzing from one school to another, collect the worst schemes from each and make them compulsory for all. How are we to know that business consultants do not do the same? It would be unethical to reveal all the secrets of the profession but this is a point on which students seem fairly entitled to reassurance. And the secret, in this instance, is perfectly simple. Among the really expert, all organizations are instantly judged by the looks of their female office staff. Vice-president A, who cannot find an attractive girl for his outer office, is most unlikely to have found anything else. His filing system can be condemned without so much as a glance. What should he do about it? Why, he should adopt the system used by Manager B, whose secretary is obviously a darling. We don't know or care what his system may be but it was the choice of a man whose discrimination has been proved.

Remember, however, that the attractiveness of the secretary must be of the right *kind*. A sultry siren is no better as an efficiency symbol (and is possibly worse) than a frumpish middle-aged spinster. Where waves of a powerful scent surge across the office, lapping against the filing cabinet and spilling into the corridor, the organization is liable to suffer. A deep V neckline can lead to a cleavage among the male staff. Such may be the effect of a swaying exit that hours can be wasted in getting to the bottom of the trouble. The office, we can safely conclude, is not the place for the more powerful manifestations of sex. Neither is it the place for the sort of sexlessness that amounts to hostility. The highest competence is associated with a bright and friendly relationship, the affection felt towards a favorite younger

sister, the sister's pride is the achievement of her favorite
elder brother, and a popular girl's trusting attitude to the
world at large. All this can be sensed in half a minute at
the reception desk. Even more quickly sensed are the

opposite signs of self-consciousness, frustration or frivolity. In the presence of a frump or a siren, the expert knows at once that the organization is in a bad way and ripe for reform.

What ought to be done — apart from installing a digital computer and apart from erecting (or demolishing) the partitions? The expert casts his mind back to the last efficient factory he saw; that, as it happens, of the Cabbage Canning Corporation, where the blonde receptionist was way above average. Demure and pretty, simply dressed and knowing everything, eager to help and quick to smile, she was obviously a girl in a thousand. Now what was the decor at Cabbage Canning? Her background, surely, had been a pastel shade of green. How would it be to begin the present reorganization with a change in color scheme?

5. PUNCTUOSITY

To UNDERSTAND the principles of Business Efficiency, as laid down by the experts, is a useful qualification for the rising executive. This qualification you now have. Principles, however, are not enough in themselves. You must also pay attention to daily practice; of which the first rule is to be there on time. The rule is of general application but is more especially vital in committee work. Nor can there be any doubt that committees are to play an increasing part in your life. There are industrial organizations, we know, in which all committees have been abolished by top-level decree. But this is a rule more easy to proclaim than enforce. In any normal society the laws of nature will apply. Committees will multiply in number and increase in size. Your own importance may even come to depend upon the number and status of the committees to which you belong. And you will achieve nothing in committee until you have learned the art of Punctuosity; an art which, at a lower level, is called Punctuality. As the following dialogue will serve to illustrate, punctuosity means rather more than being there on time. It means being there on time *and being properly briefed.*

Chairman Let's see now. Are all members present? There should be nine, I think, apart from Elmer. We have

eight. Bob, Arthur, Mike, Leslie — where is *Steve?* Yes, he's the missing man. Perhaps, Elmer, you had best give him a call. In the meanwhile, let's get down to business. May I take the Minutes of the last meeting as read? Any amendments? Right. Thank you. Now, gentlemen, I shall propose a slight change in the agenda. In view of the urgent need to make a decision on item 4 I should like to take that first, going on afterwards to items 1, 2 and 3. Item 4 concerns the alteration proposed for No. 10 Ware-house. We have all read the architect's report, perhaps with some surprise and concern. We also have before us the estimate from the engineers for the air-conditioning plant — an estimate which includes some very surprising figures. I shall say no more at present. The question is, however, do we go ahead or do we reconsider the whole scheme? A decision is urgent as affecting the whole esti-mates for the division. Far more urgent, in my opinion, than Item 1, which concerns merely the demolition of the disused fuel store so as to make more parking space. We must try and reach a decision today.

(*Enter Steve, breathless, confused and armed with the wrong file.*)

Steve My apologies, Mr. Chairman, I was delayed by some important business.

Chairman Very well, Steve. We have only just begun. You will find a copy of the agenda in front of you. What was I saying? Ah, yes. The matter is urgent and we must try to reach a decision. We are particularly glad, Steve, that you could spare the time to come. And we all realize how important your other business must be. But this matter concerns the department of which you are acting head. Perhaps we should ask your views at the outset?

Steve (*stammering*) I feel we sh-sh-should go ahead, Mr. Chairman. In view, I mean, of the urgency. (He fumbles with the file, one dealing with worker's accident compensation.)

Chairman (*surprised*) In spite of the architect's report?

Steve (*unhappily*) Yes. I mean, no. There's much to be said on either side. But the matter, as you said, is urgent.

Chairman We certainly need to make a decision. That is urgent. But the engineer's estimate comes to more than the original cost of the building. You think we should ignore those figures?

Steve (*lost*) Well, not exactly. Oh, no, certainly not. By no means.

Chairman But you consider, nevertheless, that we should go ahead?

Steve Well, we need the parking space . . . don't we?

Chairman The *parking space??*

Bob (*gently*) We are discussing Item 4, Steve. Not Item 1.

Steve Oh! I see. Yes, of course. Item 4. I didn't realize that Item 1 had been dealt with. Well, now. Item 4 . . .

Chairman (*patiently*) May I assume that you have studied the document circulated yesterday — the architect's report and the engineer's estimate?

Steve (*lying*) Of course, Mr. Chairman. Naturally. And I am as concerned as you can be over the question of cost.

Chairman Cost is only *one* aspect. The first question is whether the scheme is feasible. Is it? Or isn't it?

Steve Exactly, Mr. Chairman. That *is* the question. I couldn't agree more.

Leslie Well, sir. I for one am convinced by the report and feel that the scheme should be abandoned as uneconomic.

Arthur I can't agree with you there, Leslie. The report reads to me like nonsense.

Mike That goes for me too. Rubbish!

Chairman Remember, gentlemen, that we also have the engineer's estimate.

Mike So we have. And I suggest we call for another one from a different firm.

Leslie What if we did? And what if the new estimate were 10 per cent lower? The scheme would *still* be uneconomic. Don't you agree, Steve?

In this imaginary discussion Steve is completely at sea. He had not forgotten about the meeting, nor about the documents he would need to study. But he had allowed other matters to take his time. The result was that he was late for the meeting — perhaps three minutes late. In itself, the lateness did not matter. What was fatal was his state of disorganization. He would have done better to telephone his apologies and come ten minutes late, armed with the right file and having had five minutes to glance through the documents. The unlucky Steve will never recover his poise while the meeting lasts (the chairman will see to that) and his prestige will be at a low ebb by the time the meeting ends.

Punctuosity would seem to be the most obvious of virtues, the very foundation of ordinary competence. It is not, however, quite as simple as it seems. For the punctual person has substituted a process of subtraction for the simpler process of addition. The important meeting is at 11.45. Punctual Peter takes that as his fixed point and works backward. He must leave his office at 11.40, check his briefcase and contents at 11.30, give instruction to his deputy at 11.25, having transferred incoming telephone calls at 11.23. That leaves time to see Marty (allow ten minutes) at — say, 11.10; and Mac (allow fifteen minutes for a Scotsman) at 10.55. There are two important telephone calls to make, six and three minutes, so it is best to start dialing at 10.45. Allow fifteen minutes for reading the report and estimate (Item 4 on the agenda), so bring the file in at 10.30. That brings the normal daily staff meeting forward to 10.15 — get Bridget on to that now. Time is 8.55, which leaves one hour and twenty minutes for the day's correspondence: "Is there anything that matters? Yes, there is the memorandum from Bagworth — no time to do more than make notes on it. The letter from Doddering — that must wait. Here's *this* thing — tell them 'No,' Mary, politely but definitely 'No.' As for *that* — on the whole 'Yes.' Tell them O.K., but not before the 28th. O.K. to this note but No to that one. Put in some explanation — other commitments and so forth. File these three, no answer needed. I'll deal with these two now. Throw the rest away."

That, as we all know, is the way to do it. But the less competent Steve did it the other way. Starting at 9.00 on the stuff in his intray, he worked forward from there, with so long for this and just time for that — which brought him, unbriefed, to the meeting at 11.48. He was adding instead of subtracting, which means being late and disorganized. This is what we all know in theory but find it difficult to apply in practice. There are obstacles and many of these are women. Why? Because the housewife and mother has to work on a different wavelength. For her, things happen differently. Little Jimmy falls out of bed at 5.45 A.M. Little Joan has a sickness, which may be measles, may be tonsillitis — best keep her in bed. Rodney has overslept but must catch the school bus. Gosh, the milkman left us a pint short! There's the telephone — "Myra, dear! But how nice of you to ring up! But it was we who enjoyed having you! The recipe? Oh, it's quite simple, really, but you need an electric mixer. Can't find it now, but I'll call you back." Little Jimmy has fallen down the porch steps. Little Joan wants a drink. Is that the Baker? — tell him only *one* small brown loaf. Doesn't the vacuum cleaner work? Try giving it a kick. There! The first time that happened, I thought it was the fuse. But one kick, not *too* hard, will usually fix it. Oh, dear — Jimmy has fallen into the trashcan! Yes, he has cut himself this time. The adhesive tape is in the bathroom cupboard — no, it isn't, though — I was using some yesterday and left it in the kitchen. There's the telephone — "But, Mr. Wilkins, you *promised* to keep the pink toilet rolls in stock! Please do get some ordered. All right, six of the others." Little Joan has upset her jigsaw puzzle over the bedroom floor. Rodney!! What are you doing here? The school bus broke down? All right, I'll run you over in the car. Keep away from Joan, though, it may be infectious. Which reminds me, I must telephone the doctor. "Hello, Margie! Thanks dear, I'd love to come over at eleven. See you later!" There's the telephone — "Myra dear! Oh, I *did* give you that recipe? Well that accounts for my not being able to find it. Good of you to ring up.

Goodbye for now." Rodney! But I *told* you to keep *out* of Joan's room. What did you go in there for? You mean you *want* to catch the measles, so as to dodge your exam? Really, this is utterly disgraceful — I'll have to speak to your father about it. Come to think of it — you *had* the measles last year and can't have it again. Oh, dear — what's that? Jimmy has fallen into the trashcan *next door!*

This is the housewife's day and it cannot be organized.

There are too many factors. There is no beginning and
no agenda and no one can say when it finishes or what has
been achieved. So women work on a different wavelength
and it is no good pretending otherwise. Except for those
broken in to office routine, or those who have been un-
sexed by it, punctuality is not even an ideal. It is not something of which they see the use. The result is that the un-
punctual people in the world are numerous, which makes
the punctual minority more fussy still. From trying to be
five minutes early on principle, they go on to being ten
minutes early in practice. This so exasperates the un-
punctual that they come ten minutes late from a mere sense
of duty. In theory at least they could reach a point where
they never met at all. But in matters of unpunctuality, as
in some other affairs, a known tendency will go into reverse
after a certain point has been reached. To be five or even
ten minutes early is, or can be, a sign of efficiency. To be
half an hour early is to defeat the object of the exercise,
not saving time but wasting it. Paradoxically, it can even
end in the fussy person being actually late.

Take the instance, for example, of a traveler who is to
arrive at London Airport from New York, taking off forty
minutes later for, say, Hamburg. There is barely time to
make the connection but it can be done if one plane is on
time and the other not too strict, the customs reasonable
and the distance short. But life, as we know, is not like
that. The plane from U.S.A. comes in eleven and a half
minutes late. The customs regard the traveler's urgency as
the oldest trick of the lot. Frantically the traveler races
down endless corridors and ends, too late by the clock, at
Gate 22. But he is in time! The flight has not yet been
called. Will he take a seat, please, in the lounge. Panting

and perspiring, the traveler finds a chair. Thank goodness
the Hamburg flight has been delayed! He begins to recover his temper and breath. Next announcement comes at
6.25 P.M. (thirty-five minutes later). "P.C.A. regret to
announce that their Flight SK 734 to Hamburg has been
delayed for operational reasons. A further announcement
will be made at 7.30. Thank you." This promise is strictly
kept and the new revelation is as follows: "Here is an announcement for passengers to Hamburg holding boarding
cards XYZ. The delayed flight SK 734 has been again postponed for technical reasons. A further announcement will
be made at 8.15. Passengers who present their boarding
cards at the buffet will be given light refreshments with the
compliments of P.C.A. — the tea being dreadful and the
coffee, if anything, worse. Thank you." Announcements,
at 8.15, at 9.10, at 9.35 and at 9.55 express P.C.A.'s regret
for further delays due to psychological, sentimental,
physiological and habitual reasons respectively. Then, at
10.20, comes a final announcement. "Will passengers
booked on the delayed flight SK 734 to Hamburg please
assemble at the Inquiry Desk, where they will be given
further information regarding their flight." Once assembled
they are told that the flight has been further postponed
for meteorological reasons. There is fog over Hamburg.
So take-off will now be at 7.15 A.M. Passengers will be ac-
commodated in London and can claim their luggage on the
floor below. In order to reach the airport at 6.30, arrange-
ments will be made to call the passengers at 4.30. After
breakfast at 4.45 buses will leave the hotels at 5.15, weather
permitting. Daybreak sees the passengers back once more
in the airport lounge.

The first announcement of the new day is as follows:

"P.C.A. regret to announce that their delayed flight SK 734 is now subject to further delay for what we may now call traditional reasons. There will be a further announcement at 8.40. Thank you." By this time an eternity in limbo and a mutual hatred of P.C.A. have made the passengers friends. Nearest the traveler from the U.S.A. is a fellow victim who admits to being a P.C.A. official. "Since we have time," he says, "let's go and visit the control room." They do so and the officer in charge explains how the system works. He is faced by a semicircular wall on which all flights are shown, together with all cancellations and postponements. "Take your own flight, for example. What is it? SK 734, to Hamburg. It will be over this side. Ah, here it is . . . but, good heavens, you have missed it! It left five minutes ago!" And so it has. It went with all the other passengers at 8.25. Having only fifteen hours to spare the traveler has missed his plane!

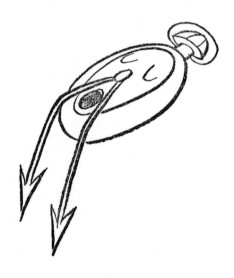

The point of this story is that being too early is no safe-
guard against being too late. It is the person with hours
to spare who misses the boat, and for the good reason that
he has time to do something else. Failure to concentrate
on the main object can be fatal. It is the ideal plan, therefore, to be a little ahead of time but not so much as to be
distracted by the temptation to do this and that — send-
ing a telegram, writing a postcard, changing some money
and having a drink. Concentration is the secret of many
types of success, punctuality included. It is a good plan to
concentrate and to gain a reputation for punctuality. Be
there on time with the right file but not conspicuously
early — for that looks inefficient in another way. If you
arrive early, having allowed for traffic delays which on this
morning were mysteriously absent, hide somewhere nearby
and stroll into the conference with just three minutes to
spare. But what if your name for punctuality is spoiled
by your subordinates? What if your office lets you down?
This is all too possible and the result is a scene of confusion. "Linda! I want that file for the Staff Committee!"

"Sorry, Mr. Scatterleigh, Miss Pelling has not yet arrived.
Would the file be in her office or yours?"

"In hers. Do we have the key?"

"Mr. Findlater has all the keys. I'll ask him to bring
them."

"Thanks, Valerie — and do hurry!"

(*five minutes later*)

"Sorry, Mr. Scatterleigh. Mr. Findlater is not yet here."

"Then what am I to do?"

"Well, Miss Lade used to have that office in Mr. Old-
man's time. She is now in the accountant's office but might

still have a key to the room Miss Pelling uses. I could ring her up."

"All right — do that. The meeting is in five minutes!"

"Very well, Mr. Scatterleigh. (*Into phone*) Give me 2573, operator, please . . . Is Miss Lade there? . . . Very well, I'll hold the line. They are fetching her to the phone, Mr. Scatterleigh." (*Long wait*) "What's that? . . . She can't be found? . . . Do you mean she hasn't come? . . . Oh, I see — she is somewhere else in the building. . . . Is that Edna speaking? I thought I recognized your voice, dear. How are you? . . . That's good. You don't happen to have seen Linda, by any chance? . . . What, you *have?* . . . She just looked in? . . . She did? . . . Well, where was she going, for heaven's sake? . . . She was? . . . Then we don't need Mama after all . . . What's that? . . . Why, I mean Miss Lade of course! We always used to call her Mama in this office — short for Marmalade! Never to be found at breakfast, you know. Fancy you not knowing that! . . . What do *you* call her then? . . . Marcia? My, that's cute. I must remember that. No more now, Edna. See you on Thursday. G'bye . . . Sorry for the delay, Mr. Scatterleigh. Linda should be on her way over."

And what of Mr. Scatterleigh by this time? Has he gone to the meeting, telephoned his excuses or died of apoplexy? The one thing certain is that he cannot arrive on time and properly briefed. And the fault is his. He has never discovered how to make other people arrive on time. And yet it is all very simple. The secret is to fix all appointments in terms of the odd minute. Tell someone to report at 10.30 and he will come at 10.36. For him and for most others, 10.30 is a little before the coffee break and means

anything up to 10.45. Call the staff meeting at 2.00 and
people will be arriving up to 2.10. For some of them, at
least, 2.00 means after lunch. More than that, all the hours
and half hours are deemed to stretch by ten minutes either
way. But fix the interview for 9.29 and the man will be
punctual. Call the meeting for 10.13 and that is when
people will be there. Tell your secretary to have the
papers for signature at 3.03, and that is the time at which
she will appear. Why? Because, first of all, the precision
used would seem to indicate a fantastically tight schedule
with time allotted to the nearest minute. There is also a
feeling of curiosity. Why should we have to be there at

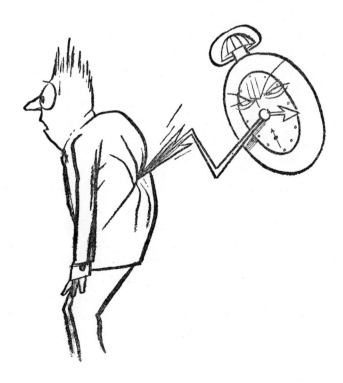

10.13 exactly? What will be happening until 10.12? Is the timing really that close? They will be there to find out. And they should then be made to realize that you have a three-minute transatlantic call booked for 10.09; and another, by the way, for 10.29. This leaves sixteen minutes for the meeting but no time for argument. An important visitor is expected, of course, at 10.32. Everyone, it is clear, must be on their toes.

Will the odd minutes lose their effect as time goes by? Will people cease to be hypnotized by 11.17 and 4.43? Will punctuality wane as the novelty is lost? Probably not. Should this happen however, the remedy is known. Introduce the half minute into your schedule. Alter the time of the staff conference from 10.13 to 10.12½ explaining that the importance of the business would seem to justify spending another thirty seconds on it. Are people going to regard this as absurd? For the time being, they may. And the niceties of timing will eventually have to disappear as impracticable. In the meanwhile, however, your assistants will have learned that thirty seconds is quite a long time. To anyone who has ever handled a live grenade it is obvious that even four seconds can seem eternal. And once this lesson has been learned it is never forgotten. The danger in war is to learn it too well, as the grenade instructor is apt to do, blowing his head off while giving his fiftieth demonstration. There is no comparable risk in time of peace, so you can safely introduce the odd minute, impressing on all that time is money and that this is as true of minutes as of hours.

For years the habit of punctuality will give you a negative advantage such as the tennis player enjoys who will never double-fault. But the day will come when punctuality is its own reward. The crucial decision is to be reached at this afternoon's meeting. Clutterbuck's scheme, which you deplore, is coming up again, backed by the idiotic Binworthy. The chairman rings up from a place three hundred miles away. "I'm sorry to tell you that I have missed my plane. There is no other until 1.45. I am bound, therefore, to be late for the meeting. Will you take the chair until I arrive? Get Dunderidge to show you the agenda. With luck I should be there by 3.15. See you then! Goodbye." Rubbing your hands, you will send for young Dunderidge. "Is this the *draft* agenda? Thank you. I see there will have to be a few changes. Item 5 had better replace Item 3 and Item 3 come after Item 8. Here are new Items 9 and 10. Otherwise — yes, that will be fine. What's that? Some members have *seen* the agenda? Oh, no they haven't. They have seen it merely in *draft*. However, it doesn't matter, there being no change in the major items for discussion. Have the agenda typed now for circulation at the meeting. Yes, that's all. Don't stutter, man. Just get on with it!"

At 2.30 precisely you will be calling the meeting to order. There will be some shuffling and whispering and Trashcan will come up with his protest.

"Not all members are present, Mr. Chairman. I feel that we should defer important business until there is a full attendance."

"But all members, Mr. Trashcan, have received a notice of meeting. I have one copy of that notice before me. It reads, I quote, 2.30 P.M. It is now 2.31 and the meeting has therefore begun. Item 1: There have been no amendments proposed so I shall take it the minutes are approved. Item 2: Matters arising?"

Trashcan   Can we be told what action has been taken as a result of the decision reached under Item 7 at the last meeting?

Acting Chairman   That matter will be dealt with under Item 9. Any other matters arising?

Trashcan   Has the secretary received any reply to the letter he wrote as instructed by the Committee — consequent, I mean, on the line we agreed to adopt after discussion on Item 8?

Acting Chairman   Look at your agenda. That reply will come up under Item 10. Any other matters arising? Very well then. Item 3: Proposals laid before this Committee in accordance with the recommendation of the Clutterbuck Report.

Trashcan   I emphatically protest, Mr. Chairman, at this attempt to deal with this important matter in the absence of Mr. Binworthy, who has been closely associated with these proposals.

Acting Chairman   I cannot accept your view that Item 3, now under discussion, is of especial importance. All the items are important — that is why they have been placed on the agenda. And some would give priority, if any, to Item 5 or Item 7. As for any member's absence, it presumably reflects that member's opinion of this Committee and its work. I feel particularly indebted to those who thought it their duty to be present. Item 3: We have had lengthy discussions on this matter at two previous meetings, that held on March 25th and again at the meeting of May 11th. At the first we called for further information, which was afterwards provided. At the second we agreed to defer the matter until the financial position was better defined. We now know what that position is. This matter cannot be deferred forever and I feel that the matter should be decided now. What we do not want, however, is to hear a repetition of all the arguments already used. I propose, therefore, to rule all such repetitions out of order. I shall assume that we have all heard the old arguments. Only new arguments are now admissible. Within these limits the question is now open to debate.

Trashcan I move that the Committee accept, in principle, the recommendations contained in the Clutterbuck Report.

Acting Chairman Is that seconded?

Fiddling I second that.

Acting Chairman Mr. Tuffleigh?

Tuffleigh I move, in amendment, that we add to the motion the words "provided that no resulting expense fall on this organization."

Mr. Stopwell I second the amendment.

Trashcan I submit, Mr. Chairman, that this is not an amendment. It negatives the motion.

Tuffleigh Not at all, sir. I am agreeing with the motion, provided only that funds come from some other source.

Acting Chairman The amendment is in order. Do you wish to speak to the amendment, Mr. Tuffleigh?

Tuffleigh Only to say this, Mr. Chairman, that our financial position does not justify expenditure on this scheme.

Acting Chairman Mr. Trashcan?

Trashcan Mr. Chairman, this is monstrous! The Clutter-buck Report is perhaps the most enlightened document ever laid before us. In it we are presented with a long-term development scheme and one which —

Acting Chairman You must speak to the amendment, Mr. Trashcan, in which the value of the scheme is not called in question. Do we have the money to spare?

Trashcan I would ask, rather, whether we can afford to hold back. Consider the advantages of —

Acting Chairman We considered them on March 25th. They were fully outlined by Mr. Binworthy.

Trashcan Consider then the criticism we shall incur — and indeed merit — if these proposals were to be abandoned.

Acting Chairman This was fully considered on May 11th.

Trashcan I protest against the way in which this vital matter is being handled.

Acting Chairman Your protest will be placed on record. Has anyone anything further to say? We can proceed then to vote on the amendment. Those in favor? Three. Those against? Two. The amendment is carried. We can proceed now to the substantive motion. Does anyone wish to speak on this? No? Then we can proceed to vote on Mr. Trashcan's motion. Those in favor? Five. Those against? None. Carried unanimously. Item 4: New contract for the supply of stationery. You will recall, gentlemen, that we called for new bids. Of these the most economical would appear to be that submitted by Keenleigh and Cut-ting. A question arises, however, about quality. Mr. Stopwell?

Stopwell   Well, sir, I have examined samples of —

(*Enter Binworthy and Dumpish*)

Binworthy   I must apologize, Mr. Chairman, for being late. A traffic holdup.

Acting Chairman (*blandly*)   Not at all. It is very good of you to spare the time. We are discussing Item 4: Supply of office stationery. Mr. Stopwell?

Stopwell   I have examined samples, as I was saying. [He goes into details] I recommend, therefore, accepting the tender of Messrs. Middling and Mugwell.

Binworthy   On a point of order, Mr. Chairman, has Item 5 been dealt with?

Acting Chairman   No, Mr. Binworthy. It comes *after* Item 4, which we are now discussing.

Binworthy   But the Clutterbuck Report?

Acting Chairman (*gently*)   Item 3? That comes *before* Item 4.

Binworthy   It was decided, you mean, *in my absence*, and that of Mr. Dumpish?

Acting Chairman (*caressingly*)   Your point of view was ably represented by Mr. Trashcan. You will be glad to hear that his motion was carried unanimously. Item 4, Mr. Stopwell?

Stopwell   I advise, sir, accepting the bid of Messrs. Middling and Mugwell.

Acting Chairman Is that agreed? Thank you. Item 5: Staff Welfare Scheme. Memorandum C, attached to the agenda and previously circulated. Mr. Dumpish?

Dumpish The improvements I wish to urge in Staff Welfare are summarized on page 32. I shall take them, if I may, in order . . .

(*Enter Chairman hastily. Acting Chairman vacates chair.*)

Chairman I do apologize, gentlemen, for being so late. I missed the aircraft which would have brought me here in time. I can honestly claim that this is, with me, a very rare occurrence. I am usually the most punctual of men, having been taught in early life that business depends upon being on time. Yes, gentlemen, as I always say, *Punctuosity Pays!*

All   Hear, hear!!

6. CHAIRMANITY

To be present and properly briefed when the meeting begins is the first rule but not the only one. In order to rise in the world through clever committee work, filling in turn the offices of Secretary, Vice-chairman and Chairman, you need a full knowledge of how committees grow, expand and ramify. The study of this subject is known to-day as Comitology. And while it should never be your object to become too involved in a merely academic re-search, you will do well to master the elements of this subject. More than that, you should follow the current trends of thought and know, at least in outline, what the most recent discoveries are. Comitology is attracting world-wide interest and few indeed can afford to ignore what has been achieved in this, the latest of the biological sciences.

Work has centered as we all know, on the Institute of Comitology, the main building of which was developed on a site between the Pentagon and the National Cemetery at Arlington, Va. There it has been found convenient to distribute research projects between departments specializ-ing respectively in History, Evolution, Current and Future Development, Comparative Chairmanity, Pathetic Hon-secticism, and International Comitology. For a full account of all that is being done in this field the reader should refer to *Theoretical and Applied Comitology, an Interim Report* edited by Peering-Snooperton and published by the Chi-cago University Press, in three volumes, in 1960. Here there is space for only the most fleeting and desultory comment, a mere random illustration of all that is being attempted. An early discovery in the History Department, for example, was that the word "Committee" was originally singular, the term being applied to ". . . a person charged to represent the interests of a lunatic. Committees are ap-pointed for those lunatics only whose mental incapacity has been established." (*Palgrave's Dictionary of Political Economy*.)

As lunatics became steadily more numerous, it was logi-

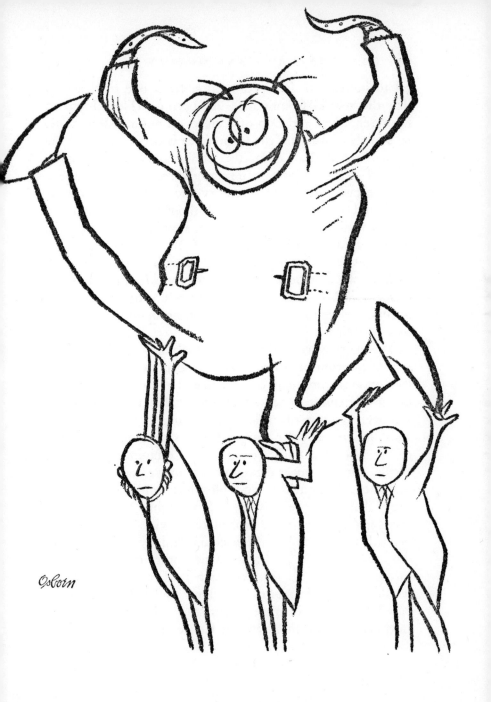

cal to increase their representation from one to three, so that the word "Committee" has become (like House of Representatives and Den of Thieves) a noun of multitude. It is in this form that the Committee is conceived; and the birth — when the Committee, as we know it, is actually formed — is of a body comprising three to five members. It is certain now that the embryonic committee numbers three and cannot well be less. Without that initial number it is impossible to elect a chairman, appoint a secretary and have any committee left. And with three actually present, effective work can be done. But what if a member, what if even two members, should be absent? It is to allow for this possibility that the first extension of membership occurs, the arguments used all centering upon the difficulty of assembling a quorum.

The classic form is thus undoubtedly a committee of five with a quorum of three. In the Institute's Department of Evolution the problems of growth and expansion are studied under the microscope. Once the problem of attendance has been temporarily solved by enlarging the Committee and allowing a wider margin for absenteeism, the process of expansion has fairly begun. The Committee grows and swells, throws out subcommittees and extends its laden branches. It flourishes and blossoms, sunlit on top and shady beneath, the loftiness of its public motions contrasting oddly with the wormlike activities which go on beneath the ground. In due course, finally, it decays and dies, scattering the seed from which other committees will spring. Familiar to the evolutionary Comitologist is the whole course of nature from seed to harvest. There is certainly no lack of material for study. Papers read at the Institute's recent International Conference shed light, for

example, on the Committee of Public Safety, the Committee for Reciprocity Information, the Committee on Interpretation of the Nationwide Marine Definition and (above all, towering in status) the American Committee for flags of necessity. By mentioning but a few of these great examples, we bring to mind the whole biological cycle from conception to adultery, from senility to death.

The basic principles of Comitology have been discovered in the Institute's Department of Evolution. Present and future trends have been described and foretold in the papers which emanate from the Department of Current and Future Developments. It is clear, nevertheless, that the most sensational progress has been in the two related fields of Comparative Chairmanity and Pathetic Honsecticism. In broad outline at least, the results of this research should be more widely known.

Students of Comparative Chairmanity have agreed to classify their work under four general headings: (I) Inanimism, (II) Blahmanism, (III) Browbeatnikism, and (IV) Confusionism. They assume that it is the object of every chairman to have his own way with the minimum of effort. Chairmen are classified, therefore, on the basis of the methods they use. Taking these methods in order, the technique of the Inanimist is to prevent the discussion becoming animated. He aims at creating a dull and deadening atmosphere in which nothing seems to matter. His simplest and probably his best trick is to be partly or totally deaf.

"Item 7. Application from Mr. Needham-Baddeley for an increase of emoluments. May I take it that this application is rejected?"

"Well, Mr. Chairman, it does seem to me that—"

"Any comments? No? Very well, then. The application is refused. Item 8 . . ."

Only a bold man with an exceptionally loud voice can attract the chairman's attention or make it clear that Item 7 is still under discussion. There are several other ways of stifling argument and the devout Inanimist will know them all.

The Blahman achieves the same result by different means. The essence of his technique is to blind the Committee with science. Facts and figures are quoted rapidly, graphs are fluttered and put aside, diagrams are waved and charts briefly displayed, technicalities mentioned and knowledge assumed. The Committee is swamped by a flood of percentages and basic trends, the members being still floundering and befogged when the meeting is adjourned. Blahmanism is common today in all fields of activity, but reaches its mystic heights among people concerned with education. The leading exponents of Blahmanism are not and never have been teachers. They are merely educationalizers, the carrion-seeking vultures who hover over the schools at various heights but with a common rapacity. They deal in purely theoretical concepts as applied to purely hypothetical pupils, but they shine in Committee. Chairmen of this type will introduce Item 14 with a little speech on these lines:

"Item 14. Report from the Subcommittee appointed to consider Dr. Fogwell's Interim Recommendations, with enclosures A to K and copies of relevant correspondence numbers I to XVII. This report, which we have all read with interest, makes it clear that achievement batteries did not, in this instance, give us as consistent a result as the ergograph test — least of all with the cerebrotonic (as opposed to the viscerotonic and somatotonic) pupils, a high percentage of these proving too extratensive to fit into the Behavioral Pattern as produced from the interquartile range and measured by the Second Stanford-Binet Testing. The statistical results are summarized at Appendix XXXIV, and illustrated in the chart placed opposite page 79. From this you can see the percentile curve for yourselves, from which (I would suggest) only one conclusion can be drawn. Is this a case, you will ask, of the Muller-Lyer Illusion? Should we have applied the Child Rorschach Responses — at least in the atypical or ambiequal cases? I think myself that we would have been wrong to do that. Our initial classification in the endomorphic, mesomorphic and ecto-morphic scales gives us, surely, sufficient data upon which to base our Octogenesis of Child Behavior. I might add that the jagged histogram offers as meaningful evidence as the coefficient of Colligation. With the evidence so incontrovertible, I assume that we shall accept the Subcommittee's Report, with Recommendations 1 to 8? Thank you. We pass now to Item 15."

The other members of the Committee have no idea, of course, what all this drivel is supposed to be about. Glimpsing successive columns of figures, equations and graphs, they are too numbed and bewildered to demand an explanation. Nor would it help them if they did, for the explanation would be just as obscure as the thing to be explained.

"Ah!" the chairman would say. "But Atomism and Behaviorism are not synonymous. Neither, for that matter, are Atomism and Wholism fundamentally opposed. So we are brought back, surely, to the same conclusion?" Knowing what the result would be, the committee members say nothing, ask nothing and dumbly acquiesce in everything. They seldom realize that any remedy exists. In point of fact, however, the Blahmanist can be foiled by Blahmanism. Another Blahman on the Committee can riposte smartly with another consignment of Blah.

With Blah meeting Blah in head-on collision, the other committee members will be more befogged than ever. But they will probably vote against the chairman if given the chance. For Blahmanism the remedy exists. Can the same be said of Browbeatnikism? It is more than doubtful. The Browbeatnik Chairman is the bullying bulldozer, the red-faced, loud-voiced man who seems on the point of apoplexy when opposed. Essence of his technique is to state or imply that the matter has been decided already, the issue not seriously in question.

"We are virtually committed to this scheme by our resolution under Item 4 taken at the last meeting."

"But, surely, Mr. Chairman, we resolved merely to ask Snatching & Wriggle to submit a rough design."

"It is late in the day to go back on our decision. Much work has been done. They could sue us for the fee payable in respect to an abandoned scheme. Then we should have to call in another firm with inevitable delay."

"But they were only to do a sketch and a preliminary estimate."

"I should say that we are committed to this scheme and to these architects. May I take that as agreed?"

"I submit, sir, that you were not empowered to commit us."

"So you are suggesting that I exceeded my brief?"

"No, sir. I merely say that we are not yet committed to this particular scheme."

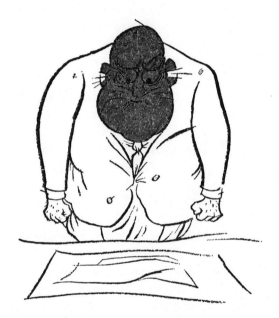

"Do you question my INTEGRITY?"

"I have said nothing about your integrity."

"You practically accuse me of dishonesty."

"No, sir, I do not."

"The question is whether I have the confidence of this committee or not. (Shouts) Am I still Chairman? (Screams)

Is my integrity in doubt? AM I TO BE INSULTED BY
EVERY NEWLY JOINED MEMBER??? (Murmured indi-
cations of confidence) Very well, then, I must ask Mr.
Barwell to withdraw his allegations."

"I made no allegation, Mr. Chairman."

"I accept your apology. I hope we can now return to
business. Having committed ourselves to the scheme which
is laid before us today it remains only to decide on certain
priorities. Two directors of Snatching & Wriggle are in
attendance and I propose now to call them in."

In Browbeatnik tactics an important part is played by
the word "integrity" which is very commonly used by
crooks. Once the objector has been made to seem a critic
of the chairman's honesty, the other members feel bound
to register sympathy, which can then be accepted as support for the policy the chairman is advocating. All objections are then swept aside and some hideous building is the
result.

In the field of Comparative Chairmanity, Confusionism
is not a recent development. Only during the last two years,
however, has there been any systematic study of its prevalence, application and effect. The Confusionist Chairman allows the meeting to lapse into chaos, no one knowing
what exactly is being discussed or even around what item
on the agenda the disagreement has arisen. Everyone is
speaking at once, no two of the speakers on the same subject and few on topics that are even vaguely related. The
resulting babel sounds something like this:

. . . But really this new parking scheme seems impos-
sibly complicated . . . I have nothing against depth advertising but I question whether we have gone to the right
firm. Why Hydden Pearce, Waders, Inc.? Why them in

particular? . . . . If we *have* to change the auditors, then
Messrs. Redynk & Blew, Inc., are the inevitable choice —
no one would dispute that . . . But why admit only blue
stickers after 9.00? . . . And this is the very type of campaign that might boomerang — virtually a plan to advertise
what we can't supply . . . Our previous auditors were too
slow — that is generally agreed — but gave good service
and knew the business backwards . . . And what are the
people with white stickers to do — sell their cars and walk?
. . . Frankly, I distrust this Company . . . You can't be
serious! Redynk & Blew, Inc., are among the oldest and
most respected firms in town. You will find them excellent.
You can't go wrong with Blew . . . That's all very well
for those with blue stickers. My concern is for those with
white . . . I don't know what you mean. Whyte's advertising bureau is not under discussion. Now, Pearce is
known to me personally. I say nothing against him, mind
you. But there is such a thing as being too clever . . . Too
clever? I never before heard it suggested that our old
auditors were too *clever*. Too hidebound, perhaps. Too
old-fashioned, maybe. But too *clever?* Their trouble was
that they wanted everything in black and white . . . But
that would be impracticable! To have all stickers in Black
and White would make it impossible for the men on the
gate. They have difficulty enough as it is — the colors are
none too distinguishable at night . . . That is exactly what
these advertising experts seem unable to learn . . . That
is just it. The old auditors couldn't adjust themselves . . .
Why should the park attendants adjust themselves? . . . I
have heard that these people were quite recently in the
red . . . What Redynks? You would be confusing them
with another firm. They have never been in the red . . .

It is not the red stickers we are discussing — they are confined to the Directors, who have their own parking place. We don't have to worry about *them* . . . But I *do* worry about them. They will give the public the wrong impression . . . Think of the lime that is tossed! . . . Advertising space . . . Audited accounts . . . parking lot . . . Lot of P.R. accounts . . . Accounts of accident . . . Accidental error . . . Error to publicize . . . Public scandal . . . Scandalous delay . . . Delay in printing . . . Printing of stickers . . . Sticklers for etiquette . . . A ticket for offending . . . Fending off inquiry . . . Inquiry into P.R. . . . Peering in the dark . . . Dark suspicions . . . Musicians? . . . No, suspicions . . . Of what?

While the babel becomes more noisy and the confusion more confused the chairman smiles benignly, interjecting an occasional question — "Are you speaking for or against the amendment?" — or putting in some acid comment — "Really, I question whether these remarks should be minuted" — so adding further obscurity to what is already obscure enough. After twenty-five minutes of babble and uproar the members will pause for breath. And at that moment the chairman suddenly bangs his hammer on the table. Amidst the breathless silence that ensues, he proclaims the sense of the meeting. "Well, we are all agreed on that item of the agenda. I propose, therefore, to move on to the next. This is a matter of some complexity, arising from a previous decision of the Committee, which I propose to consider somewhat out of sequence and about which there has already been some informal discussion. Mr. Blatherwick, I understand that you have something to say on this matter?" There is fresh uproar, lasting this time for fifteen minutes, at the end of which the chairman says: "Thank

you. With that item disposed of, we can now proceed to another . . . " After some two hours of this, the chairman brings the meeting to an end. "That concludes the agenda. Any other business? The meeting is adjourned." A few days later, the members receive copies of the neatly tabulated minutes recording the chairman's decision on each item. "The secretary does a wonderful job," they tell each other, "to make sense of it all."

While some chairmen are content with having their own way, others want their dictatorship to be generally known. It is one of the paradoxes of Comitology that, whereas the object of a Committee may be to save one individual from the responsibility of making an unpopular decision, the chairman will sometimes claim all responsibility for the decisions made. This is particularly true of any public inquiry and the process begins with the Committee's official description. It is initially worded something like this: "*A Special Committee of Inquiry set up under the authority of Congress to inquire into the Causes of Juvenile Delinquency, its prevalence at different periods and in different States, its cost to the public and to the schools, and the measures so far taken to deal with it; as also to recommend such future legislation as may tend, in the Committee's opinion, to mitigate and eventually abolish the evils resulting therefrom.*" With such a title as this, there is little likelihood of the Committee being referred to except in an abbreviated form of words. Such a body as this would probably be called the Juvenile Delinquency Committee. It is the object, therefore, of Mr. Leverage, the intended chairman (should he seek publicity) to confuse this title in advance. This is best done by adding further and disconnected objects of inquiry. The wording might be amended to read . . . "to inquire into the causes of illegal activity among children, adolescents, the feeble-minded and senile with special reference to drug addiction, pornography and blackmail, not to mention incest, mayhem and suicide, their prevalence . . . etc." By thus extending and confusing the object of the exercise, adding doubt as to whether incest is included or specifically ruled out, the newspapers are prevented from referring to the Juvenile Delinquency Committee. They have no alternative but to call it the Leverage Committee, from which will eventually come the Leverage Report. The chairman will thus have all the publicity to himself.

Closely connected with Comitology is a new subject for investigation called Subcomitology; the study of the Subcommittee. There has been some controversy over this, some doubt as to whether the subject exists. "What is Subcomitology?" asked one of our leading authorities. "It is merely Comitology as studied by the subnormal." Another scholar asked, "But is Subcomitology a Discipline? Could it be taught in the High Schools?" And to this last question, at least, we have the answer. It *is* being taught at the High Schools! There are several, indeed, at which no other subject is taught. Whether we approve or not, Subcomitology has come to stay. And, if only for that reason, the controversy that has arisen must be thought deplorable. There should be cooperation rather than rivalry between social scientists whose work is so nearly allied. For while the science of Subcomitology most certainly exists, it cannot be divorced from Comitology as a whole. We must remember, in this connection, that one function of the Subcommittee is to defeat a rival group on the Committee of which the Subcommittee is an offshoot. The party headed by A is thwarted in its honest endeavors by the faction which centers on B. It is natural, therefore, that A should propose to split up the detailed work among four Subcommittees. When this is agreed he will naturally contrive to delegate all the important work to the subcommittee of which he proposes to make himself the chairman and in which his supporters will have a majority. The B-minded people will dominate another subcommittee under B's chair-manship; one which is given an impressive title but nothing of significance to transact. This normal and everyday procedure involves the use of subcommittees as a constitutional device but is one phase, essentially, in the struggle for power as between A and B. How can we say, therefore, that the Comitologist can ignore this sort of maneuver, leaving it for the Subcomitologist to investigate? Here, surely, is a case for cooperation.

Should we agree that Subcomitology exists as distinct from Comitology but as a subject very closely allied, what are we to say of Infrasubcomitology? This is the study of the subsubcommittees which the subcommittee will often project; a study to which some research departments are nowadays wholly devoted. Is there a case for a specialization as specialized as this? No, there is not. This is the point at which common sense must intervene. To talk of Infrasubcomitology and of Subinfrasubcomitological Studies is to go a great deal too far, more especially in a university context. Professors need to be continually reminded that their work must center on the basic academic disciplines, and that specialization, beyond a certain point, becomes absurd.

From even as brief an outline as this it will be apparent that our knowledge of Comitology, both pure and applied, is steadily increasing; as is also, of course, the number of committees available for study. It would be idle to pretend that this multiplication of committees is regarded with equal satisfaction by all. An influential group of those wives who have come to describe themselves as gas widows went so far recently as to announce the discovery of an Eleventh Commandment: "Thou shalt not Commit." There can be no general sympathy, however, with so reactionary a point of view. The machinery of administration must continue to function and the study of this machinery must continue to present us with a subject for scientific investigation, as also with a career for those who cannot think what else to do. To paraphrase a wise remark made by His Royal Highness the Duke of Edinburgh, what is the use of man if science does not survive?

7. ANNUAL STATEMENT

BUSINESS executives of the past used to differ from each
other in background and education. The chief might have
come up the hard way, having originally sold newspapers or
pushed a barrow round the Bowery. His son would have
studied Greek at Yale and shown some interest in the history of art. Of the other directors, one might have begun
life as an engineer, another as a salesman in Montevideo and
a third as a professor of Economics. Of the divisional managers, one could have been in the army, another in journal-
ism and a third in the District Attorney's office. One way
and another, the Board could command a fairly wide field
of varied experience. Any given problem could be examined from the technical, legal, financial, international and
publicity angles; nor would there be lacking some aesthetic
and literary appreciation, some knowledge of society at
different levels, some grasp of politics and some knowledge
of the world. Today there is a tendency for all executives
to think alike, having graduated in the same sort of school,
studied the same subjects and risen in the same way.

The subject they have studied is Business Administration.
Taken at the postgraduate level as the sequel to a course in
history, languages, mathematics or science, a study of business theory could do no possible harm. It might even do
good, encouraging the growth of a professional attitude and

ethic. Taken at a lower level, however, its drawbacks are obvious and many; chief among them being the extent to which business graduates must think alike. It is, moreover, and of necessity, a cafeteria course in which students help themselves to small quantities of this and that — economics, accountancy, industrial psychology, statistics, automation and company law — and emerge without any real grasp of anything. Such a school will attract few people of outstanding ability. Any preference shown, therefore, for business graduates will be a deliberate selection of the mediocre. Nor is there anything in business life to encourage the individuality which this schooling may have tended to smother. Far from that, the routine recreations are as standardized as the routine work. The Corporation Octopus exacts a more complete obedience and conformity than was ever claimed by any emperor or king in modern times. And what individuality is lost is as much a loss to the Corporation as to the individual. It will pay heavily in the end for all its mental uniformities.

While a too standard training for business is thus to be deplored, much remains to be done at the postgraduate level. There is scope too for the refresher course and symposium. Whether there is much value in the research done is quite another question. There is nowadays a formidable literature of managerial science, a direct product of United States taxation. The American Corporation has a periodic urge to drain off some profits which would otherwise go to the federal treasury. One method is to set up a Foundation. Another is to launch a program of organizational research. The effect of this is to unleash the social scientists, who proceed to interview everyone on the payroll. Each in turn is asked what he does, if anything; whether he likes it and why; what he thinks of the foreman and the manager; what he finds least repulsive in the organization; whether he would like to escape if he could; whether he knows the top executives by sight and whether, having seen them, he wants to see them again. When processed, the answers can be absorbed into a complete diagram, a fusion of anatomy and electronics. This is headed *The Social System of Plant Z* and placed on the president's desk as the latest thing in Management Philosophy. What that chief executive does with it can be guessed but may not be known. Coming at the end of a tiring week, the *Social System* might well be the last straw; the point beyond which lies hysteria or homicide. Apart from proving what everybody already knows — the futility, for example, of trying to develop corporate loyalty through courses for the workers in elementary economics — such a report as this may have a special use (see Chapter 10) which is not very generally known. If we regard it merely as reading matter, however, we gain a gloomy impression of the sort of literature the modern executive is supposed to read. The mind reels at the multiplication of books intended to justify their author's promotion from assistant to associate professor. While tenure of office depends upon publication, the torrent will continue its foaming course, each wave wetter than the last. And should the Business Schools fall someday into disrepute, it will be less on account of what they teach than of what they print. Such opposition as they encounter today, however, comes from the old-fashioned scholars who believe (however mistakenly) that a university's concern is with more basic knowledge. They dare to question whether such an academic subject as "Business" has the right to exist.

This absurd attitude was illustrated some years ago by the experience of an American professor who was invited to dine at the high table of an Oxford College. There he found himself seated next to an elderly scholar who appeared to be extremely deaf. "What is your subject?" asked the old man. To this the American replied, "Business Administration." Cupping his ear with one hand and registering incredulity, the old scholar asked, "*What* did you say your subject was?" More loudly, the American professor answered, "*Business Administration!*" "*What?*" came the query, which was repeated until the professor had finally to shout. "BUSINESS ADMINISTRATION!" he yelled amidst a shocked silence at table. And at last the Oxford don showed a look of comprehension. Leaning back, he nodded slowly saying, "Oh, I see. Quite, quite. Just so." Then he leaned once more towards the American and said, almost confidentially, "You know, for a moment I thought you said 'Business Administration'!" Chuckling quietly, he turned once more to the soup, his mind now evidently set at rest.

Such incredulity as there may be about the value of Business Administration, considered as an academic subject, is not wholly unreasonable. Doubts center, for the most part, on the qualifications of those who are to do the teaching. It is widely (however mistakenly) assumed that the instructors themselves have failed in business, or else that they are people who, never having been in business, know nothing about it. Such an absurd generalization leaves out of account all those wonderful and dedicated men who have quit Wall Street for Harvard when on the very point of making millions. People in this class are known to be numerous, momentarily baffled as we may be when asked to name one. As against that, it must be conceded that the teachers of business method must at least include some whose own transactions have been uniformly disastrous. Such a one was the late Professor Aloysius Polwhittle, Ph.D., of Wisconsin, who indeed made no secret of the fact, telling his pupils that they might profit from his mistakes. He was especially eloquent on the subject of Annual Reports; mainly, it seems, because he had been asked to compile one at a crucial and indeed final stage of his business career. Few of his pupils ever forgot his lecture on this subject, coming as it did towards the end of the second semester.

He would begin by explaining that the Annual Report was originally a dull, if respectable, publication; one which contained little more than a consolidated balance sheet, an accountant's certificate and some laconic information about the date, time and place of the next General Meeting; material which came in time to be prefaced by the president's letter and followed by a brief financial narrative. Investors were assumed in those days to be shrewd and experienced

men to whom the balance sheet would itself convey a sufficient picture of the Company's affairs. In more recent
years, he would point out, stock ownership extends now to
a class of person rightly classified as illiterate and regarded,
for many practical purposes, as imbecile. For the modern
stockholder the Company must provide, and does provide,
a brightly colored, smartly illustrated brochure, printed on
art paper and bound in imitation vellum. It still includes the
consolidated balance sheet, probably as a center spread, but
this is nowadays all but lost among the artwork, portraits,
plans, diagrams, biographies and graphs. On the assumption
that mere figures will convey nothing to the reader, statistics are thus represented as colored bricks in orange and
blue. Percentages are shown as slices of cake or segments
of a dollar. The general effect is festive, innocent and gay,
well suited to the more junior groups at kindergarten. At
least one *Annual Report* has even been issued in the form
of a disk, recording the president's own verbal assurance of
the Company's prosperity. The great merit of this more
colorful treatment is that the general impression left may
be totally at variance with the facts. It was to this more
than anything else that Professor Polwhittle attributed his
own relegation to academic life.

   "Take for example," he used to say, "the firm, now dis-
solved, of Bugworthy, Gremlin & Co., tricycle manufac-
turers, in which I once held stock. Here is a copy of its
very last *Annual Report!*" He would flourish a copy of
the offending document. "Look at the cover!" The class
would glimpse a photograph of a vast factory, humming
with activity. "Look at that picture! In fact, as I afterwards discovered, Bugworthy & Gremlin owned the shed
in the left foreground. The rest of the buildings shown

were and are the property of another corporation, Konkering Chemicals, Inc., whose lot happens to adjoin. Inside, the balance sheet shows a continuing loss but this is offset by the cheerful confidence of the president's letter, as also by the statistics-made-easy. There is a piece about the Dachshundski family — father, son and grandson, all working at the same plant. There is a profile and line drawing of the executive vice-president and a glossy portrait of the president himself, taken some fifteen years before. A photograph apparently taken from the air shows the new factory; the text indicating, but only in the smallest print, that the picture is of the architect's model and that this particular scheme has been abandoned. Nothing could be more impressive, nothing more likely to create confidence." There would be a pause and then, with the voice changing almost to a scream, the shrill words: "The Company was bankrupt before the next *Annual Report* could appear!"

Letting this sink in, the Professor would now show the class another publication, as glossy as the first, full of novelty treatments and designed (as Mr. Olds once said) for the privileged millions rather than for the privileged few. "Here," he would say, "is the *Annual Report* of the Crossley Crabtree Corporation, Inc., whose automobiles had at one time the fishiest fishtails in the whole non-sensical racket. This report immediately preceded the reduction of dividend from $2.75 to $1.00. But who would guess that from reading this report? All that it says is that the advisory Management Agreement with the Motley-Mammoth Corporation had been terminated as a result of a refinancing and replanning program. Who should know

that this would mean collapse? That, nevertheless, is what it did mean. But don't think for a moment that this is the only pitfall! If some companies seem better than they are, others are better than they seem. Here, for example, is an

Interim Report from Hogsnylon Toothbrush Company, differing from similar reports only in that one discreet reference to the Company's increased provision for depreciation and depletion. I know now that this meant deliberately restricting the Company's earnings, partly by means of inventory manipulation. Companies often do this, sometimes (but not always) for tax reasons. You will observe," the Professor would remark in passing, "that I use the word 'earnings' and so avoid using the word 'profit' — a term nowadays regarded as dirty and unfit for inclusion in the business vocabulary. You must learn once and for all that there is no such thing as 'profit' — least of all, by the way, in a company like Hogsnylon. Just as some managements seek to conceal their losses, laughing them off as due to a passing downtrend or a temporary reduction in output such as must often occur during a phase of reconstruction, others are just as eager to conceal their prosperity from the stockholders, who might demand a higher dividend if they knew what the position was."

Professor Polwhittle had traveled widely in pursuit of the wealth which finally eluded him, and he would take — as an extreme instance of reportsmanship — the Chinese firm of Long See Saw, owners of tin mining concessions in Kuala Sellingtin and Lee King Bukit. Whether Long See Saw have ever actually mined tin ore — whether they would even recognize cassiterite if they were shown it — has long been a subject of doubt. It is not, in any case, on their output that the directors rely for their far from despicable emoluments. The essence of their honorable enterprise (as Kai Lung would explain) is to report on their company's prospects in alternate moods of optimism and gloom. One *Annual Report* dwells sadly on the meager

returns from the old mine and the disappointing result at
the new. A geological report reveals that any alluvial
deposit there may be will have been exhausted within the
year. There are difficulties, moreover, with the water
supply, as also with the labor force; the coolies, it would
seem, all going either Communist or sick (and occasionally
both). The Company's title to one of its concessions has
been challenged and this will undoubtedly lead to protracted and costly litigation. Inclusion of the auditor's
certificate has been postponed, the details being still under
discussion. Publication of such an Annual Report could
not fail to attract attention in the financial page of the
Willowpattern Times, where the relevant paragraph reads
as follows: —

Stories which have been current, reflecting on the indif-
ferent prospects which confront the No-Risk Association
founded by the ever-to-be-lamented Long See Saw have
lately become acceptable even to the most obtuse. This
formerly prosperous but now degraded Association would
appear to be placed in a position of no little difficulty,
with the most insurmountable obstacles placed so as to dis-
courage even the least perceptible progress towards any
conceivable goal. Reports of undoubted authenticity lay
eloquent stress on the fact that bandits and lawyers outweigh the crocodiles and that these again outnumber the
ounces of tin to be found on the scene of this Association's
ill-considered enterprise. Marketable claims to a portion
of the Association's expected earnings are no longer in
demand, the barely concealed eagerness of the vendors
being matched by a manifest reluctance on the part of
those to whom these claims have been offered at a seem-
ingly negligible price. Not even in the time of the Sage

Kings were Long See Saw Normalities regarded as a golden-bordered and safe provision for the widow and orphan, but they are now regarded with no enthusiasm even by those honorable persons among whom the most indubitably perilous transactions are a matter of practically daily occurrence. In the opinion of this degraded person, the owners of Long See Saw Normalities can best display their all but Confucian wisdom by accepting with feigned gratitude any offer, however despicable, that they may receive. While it must be conceded, among the sagacious and experienced, that this currently unpopular Association has been in comparable difficulties before, the present rescripts are of less encouraging nature than any that have previously been laid upon our humble and unworthy desk. It is predicted with confidence among persons of almost unquestionable honesty that a still more despicable sum will suffice to purchase these claims before this Year of the Cockroach comes to its not necessarily fortunate conclusion.

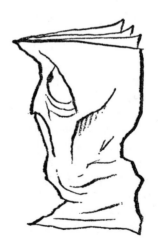

The result of publishing this report and attracting the above-quoted comment was to reduce the Company's shares to a nominal price; at which figure the Directors bought most of them in. A year later the next *Annual Report* gave a sharply contrasted picture of the Company's affairs. By then, it appeared that the output had greatly improved. More than that, a new geological and geophysical report proved that future prospects were favorable beyond example. Rich layers of alluvial tin had been located on a site where the water supply would be more than adequate for the hydraulic pump. A newly recruited labor force was exceptionally contented and loyal, most of the coolies turning out to be Methodist in religion and almost embarrassingly conservative in politics. The vexatious litigant to which the last Report referred had now accepted a modest final settlement of his claim. The auditor's certificate proved that the Company's consolidated balance sheet was not only reassuring but accurate. The result of publishing this report was to rocket the Company's shares to a boom price; at which figure the directors promptly sold them. In a company run on this principle, the Professor would conclude, it is immaterial whether the mines exist or not.

At this point in his lecture Professor Polwhittle would hasten to assure his class that no company like Long See Saw could possibly exist in the United States. He merely wished to emphasize that the tone of an *Annual Report* might reflect interests as well as facts. He would further illustrate this point with references to the 1956 *Annual Report* of Jolly, Weldone & Brothers, Inc., Brewers of Jolly Weldone Beers and Ales. In this attractive publication (of which the Professor displayed a copy) the point

of interest lay in the exceptional benevolence shown by the Company towards its executives and staff. Even a cursory study of its noncontributory Retirement Plan, its Incentive Compensation Scheme, its Christmas Bonus and Welfare Fund, its subsidized Sports Club and free Medical and Legal Advice Service would reveal a generosity far beyond anything we commonly encounter in the world of business. But Jolly, Weldone & Brothers, Inc., had little to say about all this benevolence in the Report itself. There are those who prefer to do good by stealth and both Weldone and Jolly were evidently men whose natural modesty ensured their reticence on this subject. Their *Annual Report* included no pictures of the new Country Club, golf course or swimming pool. It was only from a scrutiny of the balance sheet that the Company's benevolence could be inferred. The enormous sum allotted for administrative and development expenses had the effect of considerably reducing the dividend payable. Why was this? "I have since realized," said the Professor, "that the Company, hitherto privately owned, was about to offer its shares to the public, with valuable options offered to its directors and key personnel. By reducing its dividend the Company minimized the value of these shares, which might be expected to soar during the subsequent year. Anyone who guessed the significance of the Company's balance sheet might have done well with these shares. People with sufficient insight may well have made a handsome profit by speculation in them. Suffice to say," the Professor would conclude in tones of grief, "that I was not among them."

It was as a result of such missed opportunities that the Professor finally decided against persisting in a business career. There can be no doubt, however, that his decision was warmly acclaimed by the directors of the company with which he was last associated. This was none other than the Dismal Swamp Land Development Corporation, a fairly new enterprise which had proved uniformly unsuccessful. Many investors will remember having read something about Dismal stocks. A few may have seen photographs of the swamp itself, which is a place of unimaginable gloom situated on the southern boundary of Omega State. It is overlooked by some hills to the northwest and the essence of the development scheme was to fill up the swamp with earth obtained by leveling the hills. Technical difficulties, such as there were, arose from the fact that the hills are of granite, that the River Deepswirl lies between them and the swamp, whereas the swamp itself is believed to be bottomless. Difficulties exist, it is said, to be overcome, but those of the Dismal area are somewhat enhanced by the endemic complaints which have long been associated with the place and which provide endless scope for medical research. Protosynoperpestitis, the commonest of these illnesses (though not necessarily the worst), is extremely painful and protracted. It is quite untrue to say that it is invariably fatal — there was an instance of a patient recovering in 1911 — but it is a hindrance, undoubtedly, in developing this part of the state. There is nobody in Clueless City, nobody throughout the No-Star State, who thinks that anything can be done with Dismal Swamp. But the Corporation with which Mr. Polwhittle was working had undertaken to develop it and the work had already begun.

It was among Mr. Polwhittle's duties to draw up the Corporation's *Annual Report* for 1956; a task to which he gave considerable thought. He discovered, first of all, that general guidance was to be obtained from a magazine published for the use of Works magazine editors. It is distributed free by the Company which manufactures the special paper which the editors (it is hoped) will order. From this journal he learned, for example, that it is a common practice to publish Stockholder Statistics, classifying the investors by location, occupation, wealth, age and sex; statistics of no very obvious value save in showing that the journal's editor is up to his work. He realized that an annual report and a Works magazine are similar in appearance and editorship. He thus learned how to phrase the jubilant report of a flourishing company, lightly mentioning the Goodwill and Patent Account, the Contingent Credits, the new plant, the TV Program, and the recent award made to the corporation by the International and Panamerican Council for Aesthetic Standards in Advertising — probably a small committee formed among the Corporation's own top executives. He learned how to avoid giving undue prominence to such fatal accidents as

may have occurred at the factory. He learned how to mention, casually, without over-stressing, the action taken against the Corporation by the Federal Trade Commission under the Anti-Trust laws. He gained, altogether, a fair insight into the technique of drafting a glowingly optimistic Annual Report. His difficulty was in applying this technique to the affairs of the Dismal Swamp Land Development Corporation. Its offices were too repulsive to illustrate. Any idea of reproducing views of its real estate was abandoned with a shudder. As for including portraits of the president and directors (a furtive, shifty-eyed and sinister-looking group) it was difficult to see what useful purpose could be served. There was admittedly a scheme under which shares in the Corporation were on offer to its employees, but as none of them had taken advantage of it, there was little to say on the subject. Remained the consolidated balance sheet, recording not merely a substatial loss for the current year but a steadily increasing loss over the years preceding.

Drawing up this *Annual Report* was Mr. Polwhittle's Big Chance. Here (he would explain to his students) was a challenge. How could he tell his story in such a way as to give the shareholders a cozy sense of reassurance and hope? Dared he turn the graphs upside down? Could anything be done with colored maps, indicating the suspected presence of uranium, columbite and oil? Dared he indicate proposed highways with dotted lines, proving that swamp areas could be opened up, drained, and transformed into land of unexampled fertility? He toyed with each of these ideas in turn. At this point he would describe to his students how he kept the problem to himself, resolved that the whole credit for its solution should be his alone. The Board must be made to realize his worth. It remained only to show them what he could do.

The task proved unexpectedly difficult. Studying the annual reports issued by other companies known to be nearly bankrupt, Mr. Polwhittle found that they mostly had some one cheerful circumstance to report, as that "the net loss of $104,000 compares favorably with the net loss of $103,000 in 1953." For Dismal Swamp Land Development there seemed, by contrast, nothing to say. No one thing compared favorably with anything else. To phrase a President's Letter in vague terms of confidence was admittedly simple. But the heart of the matter, as Mr. Polwhittle realized, is the consolidated balance sheet. How could *that* be made to look better? Could something be done to increase the sum of the assets and diminish the total of the liabilities? Working night and day on the problem, Mr. Polwhittle eventually found the answer. By certain adjustments under "Prepaid expenses," by reducing the allowances for depreciation, and by placing a figure against Goodwill and other Intangibles (hitherto overvalued at $1), he brought the assets up to $22,780,000. By deferring settlement of some trade accounts, by deciding that certain compensation claims need not be paid, by adjustments in inventory and by omitting all mention of fire insurance, he found that the liabilities might be reduced (with an effort) to $22,779,500, showing a credit balance of $500 for the year; not enough perhaps to justify declaring a dividend but sufficient to suggest that the Company was solvent, with its position improving. In the belief that the auditors might be induced, when drunk, to attach their certificate to this statement — still only in draft form — Mr. Polwhittle then wrote up the rest of the report in lyrical terms. He could almost see the shares being marked up as the Company's bright prospects came to be generally understood. His final draft, as submitted to the Board, might be fairly described as a work of art, a masterpiece of its kind.

In describing his interview with the Board, Mr. Polwhittle used to create an atmosphere of pathos which is hardly to be conveyed in writing. Only his own shrill and outraged accents could really do justice to the theme. They must be imagined as lending drama to this final scene. Entering the boardroom with the deprecating modesty of one who expects congratulations and is ready to explain that he merely did his duty, Polwhittle found himself the target for a concentrated and venomous hostility. With a rare unanimity the directors glared at him as at something the cat had brought in.

"May I ask, Mr. Polwhittle," said the chairman, almost in a whisper, "whether you expect the Board to accept this — this — this document?"

"I see no reason," replied Polwhittle with dignity, "why the Board should not accept a favorable statement of the Company's position and prospects."

"You see no reason!" hissed the chairman, "You!! You don't see anything. You don't even realize what this company is for!"

"I assume," said Polwhittle, "that this company is formed for developing real estate at a profit to the stock holders."

There was a whole minute of stunned silence before the chairman spoke again.

"Why," he appealed to his colleagues, "WHY does this have to happen to ME? There are thousands of corporations this guy might have joined. Why, for heaven's sake," he suddenly screamed, "does he have to pick on US?"

"Listen, brother," said another director, whose expression of loathing was a shade less intense than that of the others. "This company has run at a loss for four years. In this, the fifth year, its losses will be heavier still. It is these losses we mean to sell — see? And the bigger the loss, the more we get for it. See?"

With his head in a whirl, Polwhittle asked how losses could thus be regarded as an asset, but the patience of the Board had been exhausted.

"Go chase yourself!" bawled the chairman. "Get out of this room before I throw you out. Get out of my sight and stay out! SCRAM!"

Mr. Polwhittle passed slowly from the room, out of the building and out of the world of business.

Explaining the incident afterwards to his students at the Business School, Professor Polwhittle outlined briefly the subsequent history of the Dismal Swamp Land Development Corporation. Following the publication of a rewritten *Annual Report*, the shares of the Corporation

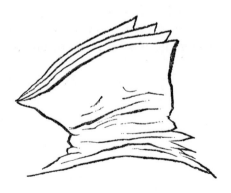

began to rise in value. There was rumor of an impending merger with the Mammoth Investment Corporation; a rumor presently confirmed in a special Report to Investors. From this it appeared that Dismal Swamp Land Development, Inc., had built up a substantial tax-loss carry forward to set against future earnings, with additional current losses capable of realization. The impressive total constituted a marketable tax shelter or umbrella. The new group resulting from this merger was thus free of taxation for a number of years and its shares rocketed to a level at which Mr. Polwhittle, had he possessed any, could have made a considerable profit.

"So you will realize," he used to conclude, "that the writing of an annual report is a specialized task, calling for experience, knowledge and care. You will realize, further, that the study of an annual report requires a comparable and perhaps even greater skill. The salient facts are often to be learned only by reading between the lines. In telling you something of my own experience I have performed the task of a signpost, which points the way but does not follow it." With these words the Professor would place the annual reports under his arm and shuffle out of the classroom; a vaguely discontented figure, not especially shabby and only relatively poor. His was not the sadness of defeat but only the wistful sense of all that might have been.

8. FUNCTION
OF FOLLY

DRAWING UP the Annual Report is only one of a hundred
tasks you may have to perform. You may do it competently, in which case the Report attracts no comment at
all. Or you may, like Polwhittle, make the sort of mistake
which lands you (as it landed him) in a School of Business
Administration. If no such disaster occurs you will
gradually gain the reputation of a Man of Ability. You
will be a man in whom people have learned to place their
trust. With your own position thus established, you will
begin to observe with surprise the incompetence of others.
The apparent folly of some will make you wonder whether
they can be of any use to the organization. Is there any
purpose they can serve? Pondering on this problem, as
well you may, you will come to ask yourself the funda-
mental questions about skill and ability. What are these
qualities and how do they differ from each other? How

do mediocre executives achieve promotion? And is disaster the invariable result?

To begin with, what is skill? Skill is the capacity to do something which is not particularly easy. Ability is the capacity to get things done, mainly through the effort and skill of other people. The violinist has skill, the conductor has to have ability as well. And ability is always in fairly short supply. It does not command the famine price of genius but it is always scarce and often unobtainable. Such is the nature of ability, however, that it often passes unnoticed. It seems quite normal, to most people, that a complex organization should run smoothly, its output steadily improving, its staff contented and its costs held down. But there is nothing normal about it. It is about as natural as a beautiful lawn, cut and rolled, with weeds eliminated and worms removed. No such lawn will happen by itself. It is the result of an initial effort and continual care, and neither weeds nor worms will go of their own accord. Somewhere in the organization's center, there will be the man responsible. Into his office will pass a sporadic procession of people who are worried, baffled or aggrieved. Out of his office will come a procession of people whose minds have been set at rest. They may not be happy but they need no longer worry. They know at least what the decision is to be.

"What am I to do with young Crabtree? He does nothing but grumble and complain."

"That is because he has too little to do. I shall transfer him next week to the transport department."

"Connie is always getting sick. Should we fire her?"

"No. Her trouble is that her boy friend, Steve, is on a public-relations course. He will be back in ten days."

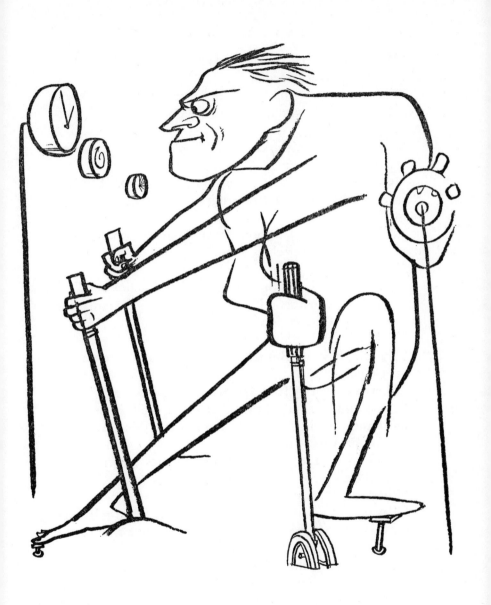

"What are we to do with Blackie's team while Number 7 Plant is being overhauled?"

"For one week they will do maintenance work on Number 3, after which they can have three days' holiday."

"Sam Deadweed is asking for his old job back, having heard it will be vacant."

"It will be vacant in October. But, Sam? No. Tell him there are jobs going at Frittering and Muddle's chemical plant."

"We have an application from Tom Wormley, who used to work in the packing shed."

"No."

"Old Bedrock is having one of his fits of depression."

"So I hear. We'll send him to represent the Group at the Atlantic City Convention."

"Phil Feverish is asking for promotion."

"He can't have it. But tell him to be at my office tomorrow at ten."

"There's been a theft of $780 from the petty cash!"

"Close all doors and all the outer gates. Tell the security chief to meet me in the boardroom in three minutes."

"Please sir, I feel unwell."

"Drink this. Lie down for ten minutes and then go home. Make up for lost time tomorrow."

"I beg to offer my resignation."

"It is not accepted. Take tomorrow off. Play golf over the weekend. See me again on Monday at nine-thirty."

Here is ability at work and the final result is to be measured as much by the things that don't happen as by the things that do. The factory is not burned down. The workers do not go on strike. Marty does not resign and

Mamie does not commit suicide. For all this the manager receives little credit, for things that don't happen are hard to assess. There is no proof, to begin with, that disaster had ever been imminent. But, whether appreciated or not, the ability is there. Fortunate is the organization of which this can be said.

In the imaginary dialogue quoted above, the essence of the ability shown is in the manager's attitude towards each problem. He decides in each case what to do next. He wastes not a minute on what has already been done. The trademark of incompetence, by contrast, is apparent from an attitude which is exactly the opposite. It is again best illustrated in dialogue:

"There has been a serious accident in the foundry. One of the men is pinned under a machine."

"Who was in charge? Joe Wittering? It would be! Why did we ever hire that man?"

"The foundations have cracked in the new workshop — one wall may collapse at any moment."

"Well, don't blame *me*. Lashup and Buttering were the engineers. I never thought much of them."

"We have proof of a Communist cell organized among the electricians."

"What has the Personnel Department been playing at? Do they expect me to do their work for them?"

"We have lost the Oldrope Contract."

"I *knew* that would happen. If only that last delivery had been on time!"

"Our output has fallen again this month."

"Not *again*? It's all the fault of the efficiency experts. We should never have called them in!"

The reaction of incompetence is always the same and the

sequence is as follows: I am not the person responsible. Whose fault is it? Why did we (or you, or they — never "I") make this mistake in the past, cause of the present mishap? If only we hadn't! Why doesn't someone own up? Why didn't someone do something? Why did I ever accept this job? From all this gibbering there emerges no word of guidance as to what anyone is to do *next*.

Ability, as contrasted with ineptitude, is relatively scarce. Nor is there any certainty that it will be used even where available. Organizations with every precaution against waste of time and money will often waste ability. One result of this is the preferment of the incompetent, which is to some extent inevitable. Where in fact avoidable, it comes about through the rejection of every candidate against whom anything can be said. A is proposed but he is said to be arty, B is suggested but he is too bold. C's name is mentioned but he is too hearty, D's dictatorial, E is too old. What about F? He is frankly too charming. And what about G? Gossip says he's a queer. As for old H, he is much too alarming. And K — we must face it — drinks far too much beer. How if we settle for L? But he's ailing. M is too deaf, or so we hear tell. Forget about N — why his memory's failing! And that goes for O, who argues too well. Shall we have P? Too caustic and clever. Q is too quiet and R is too rude. S is so silent and T talks forever. U is efficient but horribly crude. And V? Irreplaceable! Capable! Valuable! Really *too* valuable just where he is. But W? W? He'll never trouble you. Let's turn him down and return to the Quiz. Come now to X — does anyone know him? What does he look like? We can't just recall. He can't be too fat or we'd surely have noticed. He can't be too short and he can't be too tall. He can't be too stupid. He can't be too brilliant, for no one remembers a word that he said. Is he hardworking and is he resilient? Perhaps he is neither. Perhaps he is dead. To X no one can offer the slightest objection. We are none of us sure that we know him by sight. He gives rise to no jealousy, hate or affection. Appoint him at once! For this post he is right!

So X, the nonentity, is appointed. Should he thus reach the chief executive position, the result is likely to be fatal. If, however, he is merely vice-president, the situation may develop in one of several ways. Much depends, to begin with, on the quality of his negation. It often happens that the man who is negative in all other respects will conceal a positive and smoldering dislike of all those superior to him in brains, initiative, imagination and drive; which necessarily means hating practically everyone. This is the origin, as we all know, of Injelititis; that dread disease to which so many institutions succumb. But his negation may be too complete to admit of jealousy, his self-satisfaction being such as to make him the intellectual superior (in his own opinion) of everyone he meets. Where that is the case, Injelititis will never occur. It is undeniable, on the other hand, that the organization may suffer in other ways. Much could be written on this subject but our present object is different. For the stupidity of a high executive can, in some instances, prove useful. It is even postulated by some authorities that a measure of stupidity is actually essential. While we may not go quite as far as that, we cannot deny that stupidity, in some forms and in some circumstances, may well have its value. Its use depends, however, on the negation being less complete than the stupidity. Let us assume, to illustrate this point, that the new vice-president has been purely negative up to the time of his appointment. He has made no mistakes, aroused no hostilities, done nothing in fact of any kind. But he is forced now to decide on occasion between this and that. If his negation is complete and his stupidity mixed with a little cunning he will refer each decision to someone else. But he may lose something of his negation as a result of his promotion, in which case he will try to decide. With average stupidity, his decisions will mostly be wrong. But with absolute stupidity they will *all* be wrong. And that is the point at which the man thought useless can suddenly become invaluable.

In a few organizations there is to be found a man who is always right. "No," he says quietly, "that scheme is too complex. It won't work." And that is where the discussion ends. Such a man has the sort of authority, on a higher level, that Old Dick has in matters less abstruse. We all know Dick. The problem is one, let us say, of grading a consignment of raw cotton. There are two ways of doing this. One way is to submit a sample to the works laboratory. The other and quicker way is to send for Dick. By the first method a prolonged series of scientific tests will provide a formula which will lead in turn to a provisional conclusion. By the second method, Dick handles the stuff for five seconds and gives his verdict, "Second grade." And second grade it is. Heaven forbid that we should regard the laboratory test as useless (for Dick, some day, will retire) but no one would dream of disputing what Dick says. Almost as final is the verdict of that rare executive, the man who is always right. In any discussion on policy, views will be advanced and disputed, modified and opposed. Then, often enough when all present are tired of arguing, the quiet man in the corner takes his pipe out of his mouth and speaks for the first time. "I think we shall have to defer this decision until we hear from Wainwright." For the moment, he seems to speak with the authority of the ages, representing the accumulated wisdom of mankind. What he says is final. In many an organization this sage conclusion may come from one of several. In others it comes nearly always from the one: the man who is always right.

In theory, the man who is always right (where he exists) should be made the chief executive; as does occasionally happen. But he is often, in practice, too unpopular. From the point of view of his own ambition, he would do well to be wrong on every tenth occasion just to keep the rest in countenance. Failing that precaution, his unpopularity has its origin in the occasions when he has been outvoted and overruled. "Do that," he has said, "and you will lose the Berheimer account." They do it and the account is lost. He never says "I told you so!" He never refers to the matter again. But the others remember it against him just as if his prediction had been the cause of the loss. Just as people never forgive the man they have injured, neither do they readily forgive the man whose good advice they have agreed to reject. He becomes a shade less popular on each occasion; as happens to the man who correctly predicts the coming storm. So there is not, of necessity, any great future for the man who is always right. There is not, of necessity, a great future for the man with ability of any kind. Fortunate, however, is the organization in which there is someone whose instinctive verdict is so infallible. While it may do him no good, it is extremely useful to others. They have a compass, whether they look at it or not.

But the man who is always right is something of a rarity. In the more average organization there are differing opinions among people who are each of them right for much of the time. A wants to accept the lowest bid. B thinks that this would lead to higher cost in the end. C is undecided and D is sick. What is E to do? Failing a man who is always right, what if the organization contains a man who is always wrong? This brings us back to X, the newly appointed vice-president, whose stupidity, since promotion, has become more prominent than his previous nonentity. Why not ask him and then do the opposite? Where it is a simple choice between alternatives 1 and 2, this method may be infallible. Where the alternatives are three, it may serve to eliminate one of them. The system has obvious possibilities. It must depend, however, on X's being consistently wrong. For him to be merely 75 per cent wrong is not good enough. So that the appointment of X (Mr. Cipher, to use his full name) should lead at once to a scientific test of his reverse infallibility. This is done by putting problems to him which have already been solved. Mr. Haywire was tried as personnel manager and resigned at the end of six weeks, having reduced that department to chaos. Advertisement 113 was used and led to a 23 per cent reduction in sales. A finance scheme was tried and proved wildly successful up to the point when it was declared illegal. The strike which threatened last year was instigated by Mark Cyst, a welder, but abandoned, owing to the sturdy opposition of John Playfair, who drives the works locomotive. It is on these problems (of which he has no inside knowledge) that Mr. Cipher will be tested.

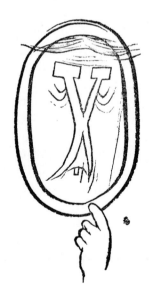

Mainstay Should Mr. Makepeace leave us (as I am told he may — but this is in strict confidence) we shall need a new personnel manager. Various names have been suggested, that of Mr. Haywire included. Have we any views on his suitability? Bob?

Bob Bedrock I think he would be worth trying. A painstaking, methodical man — quiet but popular. Yes, I think he might be a success.

Ken Kingpost I'm sorry but I don't agree. Haywire seems to me too vague and scatterbrained. He might fail completely.

Mainstay Mr. Cipher?

Cipher Well, I have known Haywire for a few months only. But he impresses me as a very responsible man. Very respectful and ready to accept advice. Yes, I think highly of Haywire. I don't see how we could find anyone better.

Mainstay Thank you. We have now to consider a new advertisement for our chief product. Copies are before us. What do you think of it?

Kingpost Very striking indeed. No risk of it not being noticed. A clever design with a telling slogan. It should be a great success.

Bedrock I wonder? It could backfire. The trademark looks too much like a swastika. One of the figures shown might offend the Irish and the wording would certainly offend the Jews.

Mainstay Mr. Cipher?

Cipher I agree with Kingpost. It has all the qualities we

need to project our public image. I think these dangers are
imaginary.

It is after Cipher has proved equally wrong on the share
incentive scheme that the testing process would become
exciting. To be wrong on one issue is normal. To be
wrong on two is not exceptional. To be wrong on three,
however, is more than a coincidence, and thenceforward
the results become conclusive.

Mainstay Our next problem concerns Mr. Mark Cyst,
our chief welder: a man known to most of us as a shop
steward, very active in union affairs. He is also a skilled
and experienced technician. We learn that he has been
offered a similar job but with higher pay at Messrs. Bone-
head & Nitwit's No. 13 Division. Are we to equal their
offer so as to retain him? Ken?

Kingpost Well, he certainly knows his job. It is a question whether we can find another man equally skilled.
Nor, if we did, would his pay be much less than Cyst is
asking. I think we should meet his demands.

Bedrock I'm not sure that we should make any special
effort to keep him. His union activities have been unhelpful and even obstructive. I should let him go.

Cipher I agree with Mr. Kingpost. Skilled technicians
are not easy to find. Cyst is an intelligent man — I've noticed that — and quite well educated. He should be a good
influence in the union. I think we should make an effort to
keep him. (*The others exchange significant glances*)

Mainstay We have a rather similar problem with Playfair,

the locomotive driver. He too has been offered better pay
elsewhere and he too has been active in union politics. Is
he worth a raise — or not? Bob?

Bedrock   Well, we must admit that he has done well. His
maintenance standards have been high. We have had no

accidents in shunting. He has never grumbled about working overtime. So I think he deserves a raise.

Kingpost   That's all very well, but drivers are fairly easy to find. We should receive half a dozen applications for his job and two or three from men with experience. Why not replace Playfair with a younger man, whose pay could be actually less?

Mainstay   Mr. Cipher?

Cipher   I think we should let him go. Playfair is a surly and outspoken fellow. I can't think he is a good influence. Don't offer him a cent more than he is getting. Not a *cent!*

Mainstay   Thank you, Mr. Cipher . . .

It is fairly clear by now that Cipher is consistent. He has been wrong five times out of five. The moment has come, therefore, to apply the final test; a problem which concerns the future.

Mainstay   Our last question this afternoon concerns the proposal to call in a firm of business consultants. We have had lengthy discussions, as you all know, with representatives of Suckerseek, Mistery and Leech. What we have now to decide is our recommendation to the Board. Shall we ask them for a full report on our organization and method? Bob?

Bedrock   It seems to me that we have largely committed ourselves already, having taken up so much of their time. I feel that we should go ahead now and engage them as consultants.

Kingpost No, Bob, we are not committed to that extent. We could pay them a small fee and say "goodbye." And that, I think, is what we should do. I am not greatly impressed with them as consultants.

Mainstay I know, Mr. Cipher, that you have another appointment in five minutes. I hope, however, that we may have your opinion on this matter before you go?

Cipher Yes, I must be going. But I feel, myself, that these consultants could give us some useful advice. I was greatly impressed by their knowledge, their experience and integrity. Each of the partners had something different to offer and the firm itself is extremely well known. Their report should prove a milestone in the history of the group. I say, let's go ahead! I'll leave you now but should add that I will be very disappointed if we withdraw at this late stage of the negotiations. This is a matter in which you can safely trust my judgment! (*exit*)

The others look at each other with all the excitement of discovery. It seems almost too good to be true. Their quest is at an end.

Mainstay So our little experiment has been a success. Five out of five!

Bedrock You know, I almost *like* Cipher!

Kingpost Well, that settles the question about those consultants. We get rid of them at once.

Mainstay Of course. I'll ring them up at once. In fairness, they should have the earliest possible warning. (*Tele-*

phones) Is that Suckerseek, Mistery and Leech? Who is that speaking? . . . Can I have a word with Mr. Suckerseek? . . . No? . . . Mr. Leech, then? . . . Really! . . . Good God! . . . Is that so? . . . Incredible! . . . But how extraordinary! . . . No bail allowed, I suppose? . . . Sure, I understand . . . very good of you, officer, to tell me all this . . . Thanks . . . Sure! . . . Thanks a lot! Goodbye . . . (*To the others*) That was a sheriff's deputy, left in charge of their office.

Bedrock   By whom? What happened?

Mainstay   They went bankrupt. Suckerseek is booked on a charge of fraud.

Kingpost   And the rest of them — are they all involved?

Mainstay   No, apparently not. Leech was arrested by the F.B.I. on a charge of treason.

Bedrock   Which implicates Mistery?

Mainstay   Oh, no. The D.A. was after him for molesting little girls.

Kingpost   So our theory about Cipher is amply confirmed!

Mainstay   Most dramatically confirmed. In Cipher, that invaluable man, we have reverse infallibility. He is our misleader and misguide, the mirror in which truth appears backwards. He is our compass with the needle pointing south. . . . Which reminds me — he should be leaving the president's office any moment now. (*Telephones*) That you, Deadshot? Mainstay here. Stop all traffic in the main avenue for the next ten minutes.

Kingpost   But *why*, Marty?

Mainstay   Don't you see, Ken? Cipher will have to cross
the avenue to get back to his office. We simply can't afford
to have an accident . . .

9. PAPERWORK

Nearing the summit of your organization, a hierarchy in which you rank now perhaps as Number Three, you will begin to realize what it means to be at the top. You will be in sole charge when others are on vacation. You will see at close range how the highest executives work and you will come to realize what their difficulties are. Chief among their problems, you will find, is one with which you have been acquainted from the start: the problem of paper. But here, at the very senior level, the problem will seem to have acquired a new dimension. Paper is no longer a nuisance but has become a nightmare. More than that, it is a brooding menace, a seething tide which can swamp and drown. On your success in dealing with it your next promotion must depend. It is a flood in which you must either sink or swim.

This flood of paper which now threatens to submerge the world is something peculiar to this century. The Hellenistic scribes who wrote on papyrus, the Chinese bureaucrats who exercised their penmanship on silk, and even the eighteenth century clerks who inscribed their civilities on rag paper with a quill pen were guiltless of anything that could be called mass production. It is our own age that has developed the swiftness of communication, the abundance of paper, the multiplication of copies and the widespread semi-literacy which are the immediate causes of the paper flood. Ease of communication has also made practicable such a degree of centralized control as was never known before. Until a century ago every large-scale and scattered organization or empire was engaged in a ceaseless struggle to make its distant units conform with central policy. For reference to headquarters there was neither the inclination nor the time. Those in positions of theoretical responsibility read with helpless dismay of provinces annexed, officials fired, branches opened and ships sold, their bleating protests coming perpetually too late. With the laying of transoceanic cables they felt for the first time that they had their agents on the leash. From about 1875 began, therefore, that tightening of the chain that has finally destroyed the effectiveness of (among other things) colonialism and diplomacy. The professional bargaining of plenipotentiaries has given place to the bickering of impotent office boys, each tied to the apron strings of a government which has never even heard the persuasions of the other side. Diplomatically, administratively, commercially, the process of centralization has been carried to its logical conclusion with all authority vested too often in a single man; and he, from overwork, quite obviously off his head.

It was inevitable that the central administration should make full use of the tools that had suddenly become available. After centuries of frustration those in authority could at last impose their policy upon the whole organization, not merely from day to day but from hour to hour. They could exact the fullest information, collate the most detailed returns, draw up the most voluminous directives and issue the most peremptory commands. Of these opportunities they have made the fullest use. But for all this they

have had to pay the price. The penalty has been that correspondence pours on them in the present flood. Surrounding themselves with executives, they battle with a rising
tide of paper. Ordinarily waist-deep in letters and memoranda, they are aware that a week's illness will bring the
high-water mark up to their chin. Rather than drown, the
key man prefers to suppress his symptoms and stay at his
desk; often with the worst results for all concerned.

After more than fifty years of tightening control, with
all initiative killed at the circumference and all leisure abolished at the top, some people have begun to ask whether
much that is now technically possible is, always and everywhere, practically wise. Some newly formed commercial
empires, the results of mergers, have preferred to avoid
centralization except for purposes of raising capital. In
others, already centralized, the question is being asked
whether control from the center may have gone too far. In
a few, a very few, the machine has been actually put into
reverse. One chain-store organization, for example, has
totally revised its system of control. Merely by deciding
that the head office should trust the branch managers, that
the branch manager should trust the girls behind the
counter, and that the girls should trust the customers, this
organization dispensed with time cards, complaint reports
and stockroom forms. It was agreed to assume that all concerned are honest; partly because they are and partly because it would still be cheaper even if they were not. In
thus eliminating 22,000,000 pieces of paper per year, weigh-
ing 105 tons, all that the directors lost was a mass of statistical information of which no use, in fact, had ever been
made. One result was an immediate reduction of staff.

Another result has been the flattering interest shown by other firms. Here is one Board that has escaped, somehow, from the toils.

In this particular instance the moment for reducing paperwork began, significantly, when the Chairman of the Board was visiting a branch store on a Saturday afternoon. Finding all the girls working overtime to complete the catalogue cards, he asked what the cards were for. "For?" repeated the supervisor blankly. "They are for filling in. Here is one, sir. You can see for yourself that it has to be filled in." "But why?" asked the chairman. No one could tell him. No one knew. No one had ever known. It was from that moment that the paper-saving movement began. What we have to realize is that nothing would have begun had the chairman stayed in his office, holding committee meetings and answering mail. He was not only visiting a minor branch store when his idea dawned — he was visiting it on a Saturday afternoon. This may serve to emphasize the basic lesson, that the highest executives can save no others until they have saved themselves. The man whose life is devoted to paperwork has lost the initiative. He is dealing with things that are brought to his notice, having ceased to notice anything for himself. He has been essentially defeated by his job.

To illustrate this point, let us compare the daily routine of two corporation presidents, whose names, purely imaginary, are Pending and Leederman. Pending arrives at the office to find his In tray piled to the height of eighteen and three quarter inches. Of this stack eleven and a half inches comprise the information that Pending has demanded, and the remainder consists of files on which his decision is asked. Hardly has he looked at the first item

before the day's mail is added. Of this additional eight inches, nearly half consists of circulars from the federal government, the top one (oddly enough) a booklet entitled *Buying Men's Suits*. It is Miscellaneous Publication No. 688, published and distributed gratuitously by the Depart-

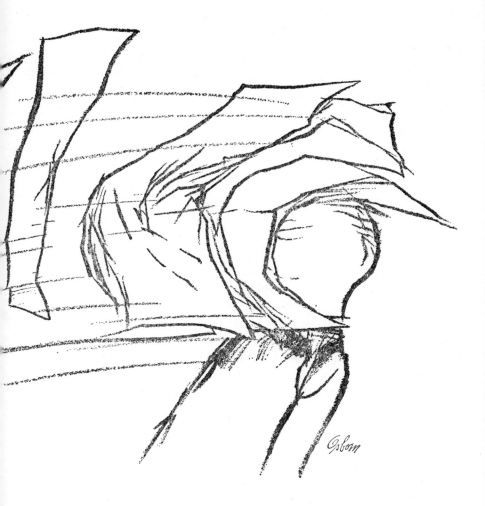

ment of Agriculture; for no apparent reason and at least requiring no reply. For circulars of this kind every office has a suitable receptacle but the rest of the mail needs answering. The process of dictation has scarcely begun when the first telephone call is received. With a staff conference

at 11.30, lasting nearly an hour, and with continual inter-
ruptions of every kind, Pending fights back against the tide
of paper. For a time it may seem that the flood is gaining
on him. With a supreme effort, however, he masters it.
The level begins to fall. With everything thrown into the
battle, with blood, sweat and tears, Pending disposes of all
the business on hand. By the time he leaves the office every
letter has been answered, every problem solved and the
In tray left empty. I have won again, he reflects as he goes
wearily to his car. He has earned his salary and doubts
whether anyone else could have done as much. But what
will happen if he gets sick? He can just cope if all goes
well. But what if it doesn't? Some day it won't.

Mr. Leederman has an outlook which is totally different.
For him the flood of correspondence is merely an interrup-
tion. Were it to occupy the day, as happens with Pending,
Leederman would think that his time had been wasted.
This outlook is reflected in his routine. His mail is opened
at 8.45 and the rule of the office is that fifty letters *must*
be dealt with by 9.15. Leederman often replies in his own
handwriting, usually at the foot of the document he has
received. His answers are laconic: "Sorry — can't be
done," "O.K. I'll be there," "I quite agree," and, occasionally, "DRIVEL!" To other letters he dictates a brief reply.
Brief it must be, for those not answered by 9.15 will have
to be answered by someone else. That is the moment at
which his dictation stops. At 9.20 there is a staff meeting
which lasts no more than ten minutes and at which outstanding problems are dealt with orally. The meeting over,
Leederman grabs the telephone and attempts to make eight
long distance calls before 9.40. He has found by experience
that the lines are more likely to be free then and that the

same calls, made later in the morning, would take twice as long. At 10.00 he quits his desk and leaves the office, beginning a leisurely tour of the factory or setting off on a visit to a branch establishment. Instead of tearing round the factory so as to get back to the office, he tears through the office work in order to have time for the factory. He greets the elderly foreman, "Hello Fred — how's it going?" "Tell me, Bill, how's that new lad shaping on No. 5?" He feels pipes to see whether they are too hot. He notices a light left on in daylight. He sees a blocked gutter and tells someone to clear it. He asks after a man's wife, whom he knows to have been ill. And all the time he is noticing things and talking, his mind is revolving round a new idea. How would it be if they installed a gantry in No. 11 shed, making a new loading point at the back? Pondering this problem, he spots a boy he has never seen before. "Who is the ginger-haired lad over there?" Later that day the awe-stricken youth will be telling his mother, "The boss actually spoke to me, asked me which school I had been at — just like as if he was interested!" If there is any trouble in Leederman's factory — and there seldom is — he sees it coming from a mile off. If the place were to catch fire, he would be the first man on the spot; a fact which everyone seems to have realized.

It is just the same at the branch establishments. Leederman always tells them when he is coming. Why? Because he says, the value of the visit lies half in the tidying-up process which precedes it — the lick of paint on the previous day. He would have achieved something even if the visit had to be canceled at the last moment. But his visits are never canceled and never even hurried. He sees everything, even the new tennis court. He has lunch in the staff canteen, taking care to meet everybody beforehand in the clubhouse. If there is a lack of leadership, a decline of loyalty, that is the time when he detects it. His theory is that the strained relationships are obvious from the way people group themselves. When he sees the branch manager at one end of the room, surrounded by a group of executives, while the rest are grouped at the other end of the room, surrounding a senior departmental head, he senses at once that there is something wrong. What precisely is wrong he may not immediately guess but he rarely leaves the place before he has found out. Should he stay the night, as he often does, the head office staff know that he will ring up at exactly 9.20 next morning. By then his mail will have been opened and his deputy will have framed fifteen or twenty questions, to each one of which the answer can be Yes or No. After five or six minutes Leederman will ring off and turn once more to the things that matter. There are people who believe that he is a very good manager indeed.

The essence of Leederman's philosophy is that the good manager retains the initiative. He does not allow himself to be penned into his office by a flood of routine business. He anticipates the questions before they have been put on paper. He foresees the difficulties before they have turned themselves into memoranda. He has gone out to meet the trouble before it has really begun. Towards thus gaining the initiative a useful first step is to rid oneself of a common misconception about what matters most. To illustrate this misconception, picture Mr. Tangible (sales manager of Steeply, Rising, Inc.) calling on Mr. Phonewright, president of the Longworthy-Faroff Corporation.

"Come in, Mr. Tangible!" says the president. "Sit down.

I'm glad to see you. Smoke? Do forgive me for one moment while I sign these letters . . . (pause, scribbling) And I have to answer this message from the works engineer — sorry! . . . (pause, more scribbling, telephone rings) "That you Henry? Oh, good! That's fine! I'll see your new plant when I get the chance — don't get much time though. What's that? Maybe you could put that in writing. Yes I see that. But what about the overheads? No, it's not that simple, Henry. There's the accountants to satisfy and the Board to convince. Phone back later when you have the figures I asked for. O.K., Henry. That will be fine. G'bye." Sorry about this, Mr. Tangible. Where was I? Yes, I had this message to answer . . . (pause, scribbling; telephone rings) . . . Bob! I was just going to ring you. Yes, yes, I heard about that. Too bad, too bad. Has she recovered? That's swell. Look, Bob, I've thought again about what we were discussing yesterday. I think it can be managed, but whoever we put in charge will have to be good. Who? No, Bob, Joe couldn't do it. Besides, he will be on another assignment. Think it over! G'bye." (Pause, scribbling; telephone rings) . . . "That you, Pete? Golf next Sunday? Good idea. Shall I ask Dave? O.K. then. Who'll be the fourth man? . . . But, look, Pete, he's not quite in our class is he? What's his handicap? . . . Guess he must have improved, but still . . . Sure, I know that! . . . Pete, I have another idea. Suppose we ask Mike? . . . etc., etc. etc." (Tangible goes quietly out of the room and borrows a telephone at the janitor's desk) . . . "All right then Pete — I'll see you Sunday. How's the family? Swell! Where were you going on vacation this year? . . . But you went there last year! Well, that's true . . . Oh, we were thinking of going to Europe . . .

Osborn

No, Mamie never went before . . . O.K. then. See you
on Sunday!" (Pause. Phonewright looks vaguely around.
Wasn't there somebody waiting to see him? Odd! Oh,
well. He scribbles afresh. Telephone rings.) "Who's
that? Oh, Mr. Tangible? Good to hear your voice! Yes,
we were very interested indeed in the heavy equipment
you have to offer . . . Right then, we'll start with two of
them, on trial . . . Yes, it will be a large order if we are
satisfied . . . Fifty, at least, and maybe a hundred by the
end of the year. What would the price be on fifty or
more? . . . Come, you could give us a better discount
than that! . . . Oh, I see . . . Well, send two of them
and we'll see. G'bye."

The misconception here is that everything should take

priority over the man who is actually present. This would make sense if Phonewright were deliberately showing Tangible where he gets off. It would be a reasonable method of indicating that Steeply, Rising, Inc., is an organization of no great repute or importance. But that is not Phonewright's motive. He is merely working on the assumption that a piece of paper is more important than a caller and a telephone more important than either. It is not that he regards Henry, Bob and Pete as top-ranking in themselves. He simply gives priority to a telephone as such, a fact which his colleagues have realized. It involves, as a habit, the risk of misjudging character and the certainty of losing business.

Where paper is concerned, public administration has had

a bad effect on business. For while the civil servant's method may be similar, his aims are different. For him, the file is the thing. Why? Because there is always the possibility of a public inquiry. At any stage of his career, questions may be asked as affecting his work. What action did he take in response to this? Was he the man responsible for recommending that? Whom did he consult before rejecting the other? So what the civil servant needs to protect himself is a file recording exactly what he has done. On receiving the application from A he laid it before his next superior B, having first obtained a legal opinion from C, which came to be embodied in Minute 43, dated March 27th. Advised by B, D then took action as follows. . . . The civil servant wants to show that he took the right decision, gave the right advice, asked the right questions and obtained the right facts before placing the right minute before the right authority. What actually *happens* is of little consequence. It is the file that has to be in order, not the people or things to which the file relates. There is a riot, we will suppose, at the prison, with two warders killed and five injured, the carpentry shop burned and ten convicts at large. When the telegram arrives the official's concern is more with the file than the prison. What action would look best for the record? How best to ensure that the blame is not fixed on the official's department? What form of inquiry will produce the most soothing report? This attitude may be inevitable among civil servants but it is unhelpful in business. For there the distribution of blame does not lessen the fact that the large order has been canceled, the client lost, the goods not up to sample and the contract awarded to another firm. In business the concern is not with the file as such but with the people and the things.

The branch manager may be fired for showing too small a yield on the capital outlay, the correctness of his procedure being no excuse. The neatness of the file will console nobody, in fact, for the losses incurred.

What is to be done about this paper flood? It is no answer to prefer the telephone to the typewriter, for while both consume time, the former does not even record what has been agreed. It is no answer to hold frequent conferences, with everyone flown there and back. Root cause of the paper torrent is the urge to overcentralize, an urge which exists in the nature of things. For centralization, up to a point, is inevitable. In so far as a chain store enjoys an advantage over a small family retail business, its greater efficiency must stem mainly from a centralized system of purchase and distribution. That there must be some control is manifest. The problem is to decide how far it should go and at what point it should be relaxed. Where should central policy give place to local initiative? No complete and final answer to this question is possible. If we are seeking criteria, however, by which to judge the point at which centralization should stop, one criterion might be the size of the head office staff in relation to the total numbers employed. Of the relevant facts this is at any rate one.

There is a strange and general reluctance to fix a normal ratio between administrative and other costs. Conceding, as we must, that businesses differ and that departures from the ideal are bound to occur, it would still seem possible to discover an acceptably economic ratio, departures from which could at least be explained. When challenged, some businessmen will mention, uncertainly, a tentative figure of 15 per cent; more as a maximum, perhaps, than as an ideal. British universities spend between 10 and 6 per cent on administration. There are allegedly fighting services in which administrative expenditure seems to dwarf all other types of expense. There is a distinction to be drawn, however, between the percentage spent on administration as a whole and the proportion of that which goes to the head office. For the first and larger percentage is an indication of general efficiency (or incompetence), the second a very rough measure of the degree in which the organization is centralized. In one very competent firm the head office staff comprises 2.34 per cent of the total employed, the proportionate expense being somewhat higher. There may well be a number of efficient firms in which about 10 per cent goes on administration and half that on the central office. In general, the greater the central demand for statistics, returns and reports, the larger must be the staff needed if only for filing them. If they are to be digested and analyzed, that means more staff and any consequent action (whether by way of praise or reproof) will mean more staff again. As collection, analysis, action and follow-up all represent successive degrees of control, the size and cost of the head office staff would seem to indicate, roughly, how much control there is. Where there is too much, it will probably cost too much. Were a perfect ratio to be established it would not be perfect in every case. There is no reason to suppose that what is perfect for a retail store chain would be perfect for (say) the Tennessee Valley Authority. The fact remains, however, that a wide comparison of staff ratios would at least provide some food for thought. If the ideal solution were not apparent, we might at least remark some departures from the norm.

While a high proportion of the paper in circulation represents an overcentralized control, a rising proportion re-

Osborn

flects nothing more than an urge to circulate. With modern duplicating methods it is as easy to provide fifty copies as ten. This being so, the human tendency is to order the larger number. Should extra copies be wanted, it is good to have them ready and relatively inexpensive to have them made. It is another human tendency, however, to distribute copies you have. It saves cupboard space for one thing. It also prevents people complaining afterwards that they were never told. So the distribution list is planted, one might say, in a fertile soil. It tends to lengthen and expand, blossom and ramify. Copies must go to all executives, all foremen, all supervisors and consultants. There must be copies for all specialists in economics, statistics, welfare, psychology, method, publicity, training and youth. There must be copies for the counsel, the doctor, the dentist, the detective and scoutmaster, store clerk and nurse. Copies must be placed on all notice boards, in all recreation rooms, in every lavatory and on every door. All, but *all* must be informed. One result of this wide distribution is to be measured in the inches of paper on every desk. Another is that nobody reads what everyone gets. Nor would anyone who did have time for anything else.

The urge to circulate, which is prevalent in business, and endemic in government, reaches its worst excesses in the field of scientific learning. In research establishments, for example, the greatest efforts are concentrated on keeping the scientists in touch with each other's work and progress. Whole departments are devoted to this, producing a copious flood of printed and mimeographed memoranda. When a research department grows beyond a certain size we are told the need for internal coordination overshadows the need for actual results. Perfect coordination is achieved only when there is nothing to coordinate. This internal problem might be regarded as serious; and so no doubt it is. Dwarfing it, however, is the problem posed by the scientific journal. For the tendency of learned periodicals to multiply has a bearing on the assumption that all periodicals should be read. Why, to begin with, should they multiply? Because each must fall, sooner or later, into the clutches of a professor (A) more fanatically jealous than the average. Under his editorship no article is accepted with which he does not agree and no book kindly reviewed other than those written by his own former

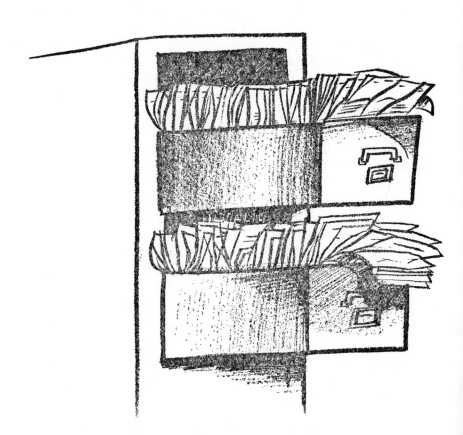

pupils. The rival professor (B) whose articles have been most consistently excluded will then, and inevitably, start another journal; one edited at first on more liberal principles. B will accept articles from all who are not actual and known adherents of A. He eventually draws the line, however, at contributions from C, whose works are confused, long, and original only in their grammar and punctuation. But C realizes by now where his remedy lies. He becomes the founder of a new and less hidebound periodical, one more open at first to new and confused ideas. There is a difficulty, in the end, however, over the articles submitted by D, who cannot even spell. But D is not to be denied access to the misprinted page. He hesitates, to be sure, before adding one more journal to the library shelves; but not for long. His duty is clear and he does not shirk it. And so the process continues until there are eighty journals or more in dentistry alone. As for the whole field of learning, the figures are staggering, and not the least so in their rate of increase. A university library may take up to 33,000 periodicals. Each learned journal will have a council, an editor, subeditors and staff. Each must involve a great deal of work. And the final result, as seems sufficiently well known, is that the few scientists who matter exchange their ideas in private correspondence. It has also been argued that the multiplication of journals is in inverse proportion to the progress made. With less time wasted on editing and reading there would be more time, possibly, in which to work and think.

Upon the desk of the executive there pours a torrent of paper and he will be judged at first on his ability to deal with it. This can be initialed as seen. This other must be referred to a higher level. Here is one that must be answered and here another that can be ignored. Refer this back as incomplete and the next as incorrect, say Yes to this and No to that, expedite one and lose the other. Have that filed and this destroyed, mark these as urgent and let those wait. Retype this as corrected and make a draft reply to that. Check by telephone whether the reply means what it says and confirm orally that you say what you mean. Total the figures again and compare them with the estimate. Verify the spelling of Vanderschnelling's name and decipher, if possible, his vice-president's signature. Ask White to call tomorrow and tell Black to chase himself. Thank Brown for his help and tell Green to pull himself together. Give Sylvia some typing to do as she looks idle and send Jean home because she looks ill. Don't let the paper mount high in the In tray. Don't let the pending get heaped on the floor. Deal with the paper, answer and file it, read it and sign it and send for some more.

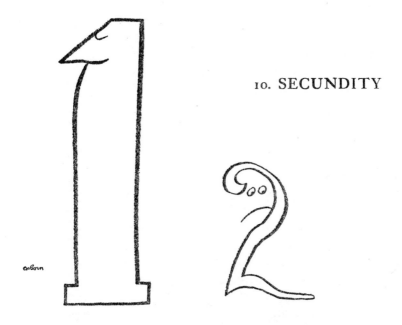

10. SECUNDITY

BEYOND all reasonable expectation, you now find the summit within reach. You stand second in the hierarchy and may soon (who knows?) be first. You will have played second fiddle before but not at this rarefied altitude. The time has come for that last great effort on which your future must depend. How to be the perfect Number Two? Here is a question demanding the most careful analysis. We are faced at the outset, however, with a problem of nomenclature. By what official title is your secundity to be defined? The problem arises because American society is so planned as to prevent the stranger from discovering, at first glance, what the pecking order is supposed to be.

FIG.

Quite early in American history there was a tendency to address any apparently prosperous stranger as "Colonel" or "Judge." Today the inflationary trend has gone further, lessening the value of the words themselves. For the honorary value of the Kentucky rank depended, after all, on the real Colonel being a man of some consequence. But Colonels have become too common. Around San Antonio, where retired Generals are to be counted in hundreds, the retired Colonel is downtrodden and shamefaced. And just as no officer can well be lower in rank than colonel, so no enlisted man can be less than master sergeant. Nor is civilian life very different. Every businessman is a manager, every journalist an editor and every teacher is a professor. At the lower level, every janitor is a superintendent and every bellhop a room clerk. Generally speaking, there are

too many Chiefs and too few Indians; a situation foreshad-
owed in *The Gondoliers* and neatly summarized in the
words of a song: "When everyone is Somebody, then no
one's anybody."

There was thus a time when "President" and "Vice-
president" were terms in restricted use; as, in the federal
constitution, they still are. But vice-presidents have been
tending to multiply, the larger universities having up to
about six apiece and the larger corporations up to about
fifteen. And even the Corporation President has lost something of his lonely eminence, most of his immediate colleagues turning out to be president of a subsidiary company. So our terms of status are apt to prove misleading
and fluid. Behind their imprecisions there loom, however,
the hard facts of life. In nearly every big organization
there is a Number One. There is also, and almost as inevitably, a Number Two. They might be, respectively, the
President and the Executive Vice-president, or they might
be called something else; but there they are and have always been, and there presumably they will always be. In
primitive societies the family group is headed by the father
or the grandfather, "the old man" (as a ship's master is still
called) to whom his eldest son stands as Number Two,
deputy, and presumed successor. All human authority has
this paternal origin, being based on wonder, affection and
fear; wonder felt by a child when witnessing his father's
skill, affection for a protector who is interested in securing
the child's survival, and fear of the punishment which the
father, as teacher, is bound to inflict. The office of Number Two, or eldest (or, alternatively, ablest) son has thus
a respectable antiquity.

But does every organization have an acknowledged

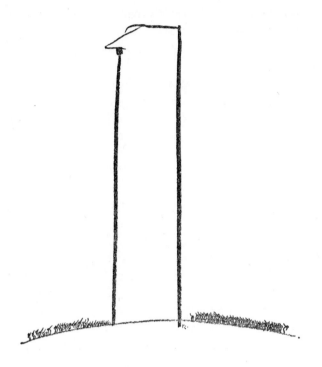

Number Two? No, there is a significant exception. In a political despotism or dictatorship there is no real deputy and no named successor. For the whole strength of the regime rests on the assumption that the current ruler is impossible to replace. After all, an effective deputy makes the ruler less indispensable. A known successor makes him less secure. It is part of the technique, therefore, of dictatorship to leave the second throne unfilled. Instead of Number Two there are several people in competition, the position of each weakened by the jealousy of the rest. Nor is dictatorship unknown in commerce and industry. There have been corporations ruled in much the same way and usually with the same result; namely that the organization lasts no longer than the man. The normal preference of mankind is for institutions of greater stability, for types of government which can survive a single bullet, for industrial empires which can survive a single heart attack. So that industrial dictatorships are more the exception than the rule.

Another exception to the normal is to be found where the Number Two is really the Number One. The whisper goes round that Mr. Lurking is the man to see if you want results — not Mr. Roger de Coverley, president though he

may be. This sort of situation is not uncommon. There are men like Mr. Lurking who hunger for power but not for office and they sometimes contrive to join forces with someone like Coverley, who longs for office but not for power. It was thus at one time the German Army custom to select a Chief of Staff with meticulous care, appointing his Commander in Chief as a careless afterthought. There are examples, moreover, of such an inverted partnership proving successful, as it might often prove in a society merely of men. Among a celibate priesthood, as with a Cardinal and his confessor, this arrangement may often work well. But where one man is married there is an element of instability in the relationship; and where both are married there are two. The married chief who is dominated by his Number Two is also likely to be dominated by his wife; and she, resenting a rival's influence, will urge her husband to assert himself. Number Two's wife may be more submissive to Number Two but her grievance will lie in the almost insufferable airs of superiority assumed by the wife of Number One. The influence of the Bishop's lady in Trollope's novel was greater than that of the Bishop's chaplain, not merely because she was more formidable but because she was more constantly at the Bishop's side. So it is in real life. And even were both men bachelors, who can guarantee that they will so remain? Where a single red-haired and pert-nosed secretary can bring about an internal revolution, the situation lacks stability. The pyramid stands better with its apex at the top.

Taking, then, the normal and preferable situation where Number One is actually as well as theoretically in charge, we must now consider the position of Number Two. Our temptation at the outset is to conclude that all Number

Two's are alike. It is so easy to picture the ideal Number Two — old Tom, old Dick or old Harry, so *reliable*, so quietly efficient, always there when wanted, so tactfully absent when not required, so kind to the office staff and such a delightful uncle to Number One's children. But such incidental functions as these must not be allowed to cloud our vision. Number Two's are *not* all the same. Some are self-effacing and obscure, others are mysterious and secretive. There is the Number Two who is genial but evasive and the opposite type who is negative and dumb. Some are effusively cooperative but foiled, it would seem, by the opposition of the Board. Others are obstructive and

surly until outflanked by an appeal to higher authority. Number Two's might seem, in fact, to offer an infinite variety in temperament and outlook. They actually fall, however, into two basic categories; those (A) who are content to be Number Two and those (B) who want to become Number One. It might not be easy to draw a firm line as between the one category and the other — for some individuals are to be found in a state of transition — but the categories exist and the majority of Number Two's can be placed in one or the other.

The inevitable and eternal Number Two's, who lack, and perhaps have always lacked, any higher ambition, are easily distinguishable. They reveal a slight wandering of interest, a preoccupation with things not strictly within the organization. They talk of school boards, local politics, country clubs and the Chamber of Commerce. Their homes reveal an assumption that they will always be there — as in the transplanting of grown trees and the concreting of the drive. They are as active as ever, mind you — never more so — and never (well, hardly ever) late at the office. But they have passed the age of ambition and have begun to take a pride, rather, in the progress of their children; in their son's success at college or their married daughter's firstborn. There is a settled, comfortable look about the predestined Number Two. He is to be identified more by that than by anything he says. From force of habit he may even go on talking of promotion but his words are belied by his appearance. It may be years, however, after his hopes have faded before he admits, even to himself, that he likes being Number Two and that he will never now be anything else. What is obvious to others may not be obvious to him.

There is an art in being the contented Number Two, whether as one predestined from the start or as one whose role has been thrust upon him. It is the art, essentially, of identifying oneself with a hero. At the cinema or before the television screen the normal person will readily identify himself with the hero of the moment. He does not visualize the Western Set at the Studio and the director ordering a tenth retake of the first sequence. He does not wonder why people should always fall when hit and nevertheless rise unhurt. He just clenches his fists or allows his hand to hover over an imaginary holster, seeing the hero's prowess as his own. The ideal Number Two makes Number One his hero and assumes for himself a share of the drama. It is "we" who take the decision and "we" who quell the absurd proposals put forward at the Board Meeting. "Number One knows all that goes on," says Number Two. "You can't fool *him*. He knows all the answers." But the tone of his admiration cannot hide from us the fact that Number Two has projected himself into the part. Number One's achievement has become partly his. And Number Two's (A) although they may differ at the outset, tend to become alike as time goes on. It is thus the duty of a Chief of Staff to write in the style of his Commander in Chief, so choosing his words that the dispatch hardly needs alteration. The ideal Number Two speaks with the voice of his chief and has no separate views of his own.

Come now to Category B, the probably larger group of Number Two's whose ambition is to be Number One. These executives can be divided into three groups, (I) (II) and (III). Those in Group I were all appointed *since* Number One. Chosen by Number One himself from among the departmental heads, this type of deputy seems relatively young and optimistic, never (he says) having expected such promotion and never having held such high office before. "Gee!" he will exclaim, "but it's great to work under a guy like Alan Topleigh! I learn something new every day. He's a swell guy — and does he know his stuff! I guess I know when I'm lucky." Bubbling over with devotion, especially when within earshot of Mrs. Topleigh, Bob Upton is obviously a Coming Man. He can't think why the chief should have picked on *him*, with so many good men to choose from, but there it is. Alan shall never regret his choice, not if Bob can help it. When Alan is away at a convention, Bob shines as deputy. "No," he says, "I don't think that is the decision that Alan would have made." "Yes," he admits, "that's pretty much in line with our policy." "As for that last item," he concludes, "I guess that had better wait until Alan gets back." And when Alan Topleigh talks about retirement, it is Bob who leads the deputation that implores him to stay on. "Maybe you need a vacation, sir, but we all want you back here at your desk. We still need you and we can't believe you're through." Everyone agrees that Bob Upton is a great guy and that his star is in the ascendant.

In Group II are the Number Two's who were appointed *before* Number One assumed his present post. Each was the choice of Number One's predecessor. Mark Waydown is a good example of a Number Two (BII). He is the very best type of executive, efficient, cooperative and popular. Rumor has it that the Board took a chance on the present Number One, Mr. Picton Young, Jr., and would never have done so had they not been able to rely on Waydown — the ideal man to help a chief whose experience (at that time) was hardly sufficient. And no one can deny that Mark ("Daddy" to the juniors) has done a splendid job. He is not really so much older than Number One but he often seems elderly by comparison — and just a little in-clined to fuss. But the organization would be nowhere, simply *nowhere* without him. If anyone knows the busi-ness, it is he. He knows everyone by name and is always ready with advice or help. It is he who remembers that a scheme like the one under discussion was tried before in 1937. If there is a complex job to do, Mark is the man to tackle it. He takes a simple pride in the way he is trusted by the Board. No one has ever questioned his loyalty to Number One, even though some believe him to be the abler man of the two. "Leave it to Mark," says Number One, and the job, whatever it is, will be finished in time. If the

corporation output can be said to depend on any one individual, Mark would be that man; or so most people think.
He is more than valuable, he is *essential.*

In the same category and group as Mark Waydown but
in a different industry is Carveth Carping, unquestionably
one of the ablest executives in the Bellectronics business.
Of Carping's ability there can be no doubt at all. He
would have been president if Victor I. Peake had not happened to be available. A little older than Mark Waydown
and looking older than he is, Carveth has never been more
than civil to Victor. Eight years his junior, the president
makes a show of friendly informality but it deceives nobody. As for Carveth, he overflows with unspoken criticism. Asked about the Company's policy, he outlines the

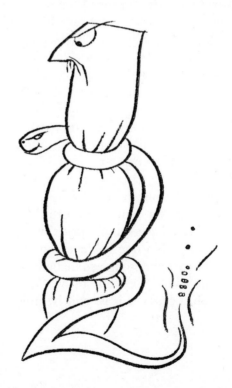

current plan for development, shrugs his shoulders and adds, after a slight pause, "Whether this scheme is the best we can do . . . well, time will show. Some of us have sometimes — oh, well, it doesn't matter now. You know Peake, of course? A great guy, yes sir! I don't know how he does it — I really don't!" He is often heard to say, "I don't know how he does it," and there is just enough ambiguity about this to create despondency. Without uttering a word which could be called disloyal, Carveth throws doubt on each decision the president takes. "If we didn't *trust* the chief as we do, we might *almost* think he had misjudged the market trend, but I guess he must know what he's doing. He has a sort of intuition, and that's more valuable, I daresay, than mere experience. We shall see . . ." Carveth is a master of pregnant silence — he could have taken his degree in it — and his raised eyebrows convey more distrust than words could express. From all Carveth omits to say, it is obvious that Peake's failure is complete.

Last of all, there is Group III, comprising former Number One's, brought into the organization as the result of a merger. There is Brent Boughtover, for example, who became Number Two of the Giantsquid Corporation when his own company (Frankleigh, Tottering & Co.) was absorbed in 1960. Relations between the president and Brent are too polite to be convincing. "Let's ask Brent's opinion before we go any further," says Silas Summit. "Oh, no, Silas," says Brent, "your judgment is best — I would rather be guided by you." "Thank you, Brent, but you have more experience in this particular field." "I wouldn't say that, Silas — I guess you know more than any of us." "You are too modest, Brent," etc. etc. So the discussion goes on, Silas devoutly wishing that Brent were not there, and Brent wishing as fervently that he were somewhere else. The Number One reduced in rank presents a frequent problem in the world of business and one to which there is usually only one solution: Brent's retirement or transfer. If we analyze and compare the present position of these four representative Numbers Two's, we realize at once that Bob Upton is the only one certain of promotion. In the ordinary way, we should expect him to leave shortly in order to accept the presidency of a smaller concern in the same line of business. This appointment will be on Alan Topleigh's recommendation, his private letter emphasizing that Bob is the best man he has ever trained. Three years later, Topleigh will retire and Bob will be his obvious successor. No such good fortune awaits Mark Waydown, who is indispensable (as Number Two). Picton Young will never release him. Should Mark put in for the top post elsewhere, at his wife's insistence, Picton's letter of recommendation will lay stress on his loyalty and competence while subtly throwing doubt on his fitness to be Number One. "As actual head of an organization, Mr. Waydown is untried, but of this I am certain, that he will always do his utmost." With this kind of support, Mark is sure of second place on any short list, and second will remain unless the man chosen should actually burst a blood vessel and drop dead on being offered the post. The question often asked is whether Mark really wants more responsibility than he has. Who can tell? Certainly not Mark himself, in whom disappointment and relief are nicely balanced. The truth is, maybe, that he was more ambitious to begin with and is less ambitious now. But rejecting an applicant is very much a matter of habit. Whoever has been rejected once will usually be rejected again. And whoever has been passed over once, the appointment going to a younger man, will certainly be passed over again. To appoint him on a later occasion would be tantamount to admitting that the earlier rejection was a mistake; which is absurd. So Mark's chances of promotion are in inverse proportion to his present usefulness. His chances are dwindling and will presently vanish.

But Mark's chances, slight as they are, look hopeful when compared with those of Carveth Carping. The position of these two men is basically the same (BII), each having seen a younger man preferred. It is their reaction that has been different. To the man passed over, two obvious courses are open. He can show by his loyal co-operation that there is no vice in him. Or else he can show, by proof of superior intelligence, that the decision against him was unquestionably wrong. Either course is fatal but the latter more immediately so. For the mutual dislike between Peake and Carping must produce a state of dead-lock. Carping would go, as Number One, to a smaller company, but Peake will never support his claim. In theory, Peake should be anxious to get rid of him and so indeed he is. But this anxiety is seldom so strongly felt as to produce a glowing testimonial. Carping's actual promotion is too high a price to pay for his removal. The mutual loathing felt for each other by Peake and Carping is the force, in fact, which keeps them together. And were Peake to find the situation intolerable he would almost certainly frustrate himself in a different way. For his letters of support would become too effusive as well as too numerous. Beyond a certain point enthusiasm arouses suspicion. "If this guy is really such a ball of fire why is

Peake so keen to get rid of him?" "Maybe he makes Peake
feel small." "In that case we can't give much weight to
Peake's recommendation. Let's take another look at Rat-
race again, the Number Two at Savage, Striving, Inc." So
Carping is not even placed. And the more consistently he
is proved right, the farther down the list does his name
appear. Who wants a man who is always saying "I told you
so"? In the ordinary course of events Carping is doomed
to frustration. Had he been made Number One in the
first place he would have been as good as Peake or better.
But disappointment has spoiled his character as well as his
prospects. He is no longer in the hunt.

And what of Brent Boughtover? His prospects are relatively good. There is a certain fraternity among Number
One's, a feeling of club membership. Once in, you are al-

ways in, at least for some purposes; and, once out, you
stand a fair chance of readmission. If Brent is not too near
the age of retirement he will have Summit's help towards
a new position as Number One. It will not do to have former Number One's on the labor market. It lowers the
status of the others, serving as a reminder of what can
befall any one of them. There is an unspoken rule that the
man displaced should, if possible, be hauled back onto the
raft. What is least desirable is to have Brent still there as
Number Two.

From this study of Number Two's (A) who are content
as they are, and Number Two's (B) who long for promotion, it will be apparent that the role to avoid is that of a
Number Two (B) to whom promotion is denied. So much
is clear enough: but what if this is the role that has been
thrust upon you? It can happen to any of us. So let the
reader suppose, for a minute, that it has happened to him.
You have been rejected for the top post, let us imagine,
and the man chosen is six years your junior. You might
yourself be content, in time, to remain Number Two, but
your wife is NOT content to be the Number Two wife.
She has begun to give you the pitying glance which is reserved for the world's predestined Number Two's. Your
daughter has been heard to refer to you as "Poor old Pop."
The situation is serious, not to say critical, and it is a case
of Now or Never. What are you to do?

The starting point for your pondering is this question:
WERE THEY RIGHT TO PASS YOU OVER? So far, in discussing the position of Mark Waydown, Carveth Carping,
Bob Upton and Brent Boughtover, we have assumed that
all these Number Two's are capable, or were once capable,
of being Number One. There are many Number Two's

of whom this can fairly be said. But there are others, equally ambitious and undoubtedly able, who would fail if promoted. Nor shall we understand the essential character of a Number Two unless we can analyze his shortcomings. What distinguishes the natural Number One from the inevitable but frustrated Number Two? You are too modest to press your own claims so we shall ask your wife whether the Board was right to reject you. Suppose that her reply is on these lines:

"Right? Are you crazy? Everyone knows that Mike is the better man. He has been the brains of the business for years. After all, he ought to understand the trade, having joined the staff in 1946, just when he came out of the Navy. How he worked in those early days, when we were first married! He used to work all night so as to have the answer ready when the boss wanted some information. Mike is a worker all right. And then, everyone likes him. Yes, *everyone.* There is never a grumble if Mike says that people must stay on at the office. They know that it must be necessary, and they know that he'll be the last to leave. Though I say it myself, Mike is the very best man they could have chosen. And what do they do? They find this Upward fellow and his cheap-looking wife. It's the craziest thing they ever did."

Let us suppose that all she says is true. You are all she thinks and more. But we still have no proof that you are Number One material. *Are you?* It is your own answer to this question that is important. You must believe in yourself before others can believe in you. Your own verdict comes first and it may be final. Newspapers sometimes carry self-marking questionnaires in which people are invited to assess their own qualities, often on the basis of twenty questions or more. For you, for the man who has already come so far towards success, for a perfectly competent Number Two, there are only three questions, and they are as follows:

Question One When you have a cold or high temperature, on what day of the week does it begin? Think back carefully. Maybe you will answer, "Well it might begin any day, I guess. Can't say I've really noticed." If that is your answer, Number Two is your right level. For the predestined Number One will answer without hesitation: "All my ailments begin on Friday afternoon and I always recover by Monday morning." The point is that a Number Two destined to be Number One must never get sick, or not at least until years after his promotion. Everyone else can have influenza if they like and can have it during the same week, as they often do, but that makes it all the more vital that you should be there. And at your desk you will be found, let the epidemic be what it may. But can the onset of an illness be thus controlled by the patient? It certainly can. You make no deliberate effort but in the natural boss (if you are one) the ailment is subconsciously held in check. There is some internal mechanism which keeps the germs on the leash from Monday through Friday. "You can't be ill now," it whispers. "There's the staff meeting this afternoon." "There's the lunch for Senator Dimwit," it hisses. "You can't begin sneezing yet." This built-in mechanism works perfectly until Friday midday. Although no longer in top form, you deal with all the urgent business and begin signing the outgoing mail at about 3.30. It is then that your confidential stenographer observes for the first time that you are not looking well.

As she comments on this, using that tone of motherly solicitude which she was made to rehearse at the secretarial college, you sneeze. "Oh, dear, Mr. Toplevel, I do believe you have a touch of flu." You realize that she is (as always) right, and the internal mechanism suddenly lets go, muttering, "It's O.K. now. Give it the works! You can be as sick as you like — until Sunday midnight." Away you stagger, hardly able to stand upright. You retire to bed with a hot whisky and lemon. Your temperature reaches 102° that night and you wonder whether you have a fifty-fifty chance of survival. None can be so desperately ill as those whose general health is excellent. By Saturday midday you send for your lawyer (who can't be found, having gone fishing), saying that you must alter your will — a matter of some small bequest to a medical research foundation. By Saturday night you are on the point of death. On Sunday morning you are recovering. During the afternoon you are convalescent. And by Monday morning you are back at your desk and perfectly well. The existence or absence of this internal mechanism is a simple question of fact. If you don't have it, you are not of the stuff of which Number One's are made. You have it? Yes? Then go on to the next question.

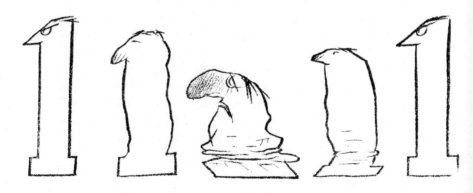

Question Two Are you prepared to do whatever the other fellows can't or won't? In theory, everyone on the payroll is there to do what he or she is told. In practice, however, they do as they like. One has a taste for public relations and another likes to file documents where they can never again be found. One loves to draw up organization charts and another goes round switching off the lights. But there is one man who cannot do what he likes and that is Number One. For on him devolves, in addition to his normal work, the job that is left over; and no one can guess what that is going to be. It may be working out the vacation roster or it may be choosing the paint. It might be checking the gas consumption and then again it might be testing the fire drill. It could be having the windows cleaned or it could be mending the fuse. But whatever it may chance to be, there is nobody left to do it — except Number One. It is what no one else will do that falls, in the end, to him. Are you prepared for this and cheerfully confident? You are? Then go on to the last question — which is not so easy.

Question Three ARE YOU PREPARED TO FIRE JOE WITTERING? You know him, of course. Every organization has or has had a Joe Wittering. He is quite honest and very generally liked and is one of the most well-meaning fellows alive. He bumbles around harmlessly with unanswered letters in his pocket, breakfast smears on his tie, cigarette ash on his trousers and a vacant smile on his face. Joe is known to everybody as a kindly old muddler with a popular wife and five children at school. There might be a case for retaining Joe but we'll suppose that there isn't. In another organization he might have been useful, even invaluable, as the man who is always wrong (see Chapter 8). But times are hard, competition is keen, money is scarce and we can't afford to make any more mistakes. Joe has to be fired. As Number One, it is your job and no one else's to send for Joe and say: "You are not good enough for this company and I am abolishing your post as from October 1st. You have until then to find yourself another job. Short of perjury, I shall do what I can for you." His face will go white and his hands will tremble. He will stammer something about his past work, about his wife and kids, to which you will reply: "I'm sorry, Joe, but my decision is final." You are ready to do that? But this is not the whole of the test. For, having looked Joe Wittering in the eyes and said, "You're fired," you have to go home and sleep soundly, not having given the matter another thought. To be a good Number Two (which you are) you need knowledge, skill, ability and tact. All these you need as Number One but with something else, that

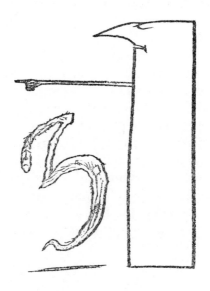

mean streak, that touch of ruthlessness which distinguishes
the man at the top. It may be a General's duty to order the
blowing of a bridge, knowing that some of his own troops
are still on the other side. It may fall to a ship's commander
to close the watertight bulkhead, with stokers trapped
beyond. Nor is this sort of decision taken with cinematic
emotion. It is done calmly and coldly, leaving only that
permanently changed expression of the mouth and the
eyes. Do you pass that final test in its lesser peacetime
form? It is not merely a question, remember, of firing Joe
Wittering. You must sleep soundly afterwards. There
must be no wondering, "Did I do the right thing?" — no
guesses as to what the Witterings will do, but an instant
switching to the next problem; which may indeed be the
firing of somebody else.

We shall suppose now that you have given the right
answer to each of the three vital questions. All your ailments happen between Friday afternoon and Monday
morning. You are able and ready to do whatever job is
left over. And you are prepared to fire Joe Wittering.
With all your experience and ability and with the three
additional qualities that mark you out for leadership, you
have nevertheless been turned down. With a barely credi-
ble want of common sense, the Board has appointed a
younger man as chief, leaving you as Number Two.
Human failings being what they are, this sad fate could
befall anyone; and now, after years of successful work,
it has happened to you. The new Number One has arrived and you have bade him welcome on behalf of the
salaried staff. You have added your own warm congratulations, noting inwardly that his hair is thinning and that his
suit is badly tailored. Your wife considers that Number

One's wife is older than she pretends to be and that her taste in dress is almost (well, let's face it) *dowdy*. The ceremonies are over and now the question is — what are you to do next?

Until very recently there would have been no answer to this question. The only hope for Number Two, we should have had to admit, lies in the possibility of Number One having a long and serious illness, leaving Number Two well established by the time Number One actually resigns or dies. But this sort of illness is, in fact, extremely unlikely. In the words of the proverb, a watched pot never boils. The person who is to benefit from an annuity will live forever. It is no good waiting for Number One to fall sick. The better policy is to maneuver him out of the way. It was once believed that people could be forced to retire by a combination of form-filling and air travel. Sound as it was in its day, the method is no longer effective. Nor will this surprise anyone who has ever used insecticide. In the first year, as we know, an insecticide will produce some results; not killing the mosquitoes, perhaps, but definitely giving them the sense of being unwanted. In the second year their feelings are unhurt — they are used to it. In the third year they like it. And in the fourth year they quite possibly cannot live without it. So it is with our high executives. They have come to look upon aircraft with a tolerance bordering on affection. So the need arises for some other means of discouraging those senior to us. It is just such a secret that is now to be revealed for the first time.

This most up-to-date form of Number-One-Removal involves the application of Management Science. If you, as Number Two, are unfamiliar with Management Science, your first move should be to hire a Ph.D. from, say, California. Experts in this field are numerous and cheap, so that there should be no difficulty in recruiting a Management Scientist from a Business School. Suppose that the one chosen is Dr. U. C. L. Angeles, whose wife, Ann Utherwon, is herself a specialist in Behavior. You persuade Number One to allow the Head Office to be made the subject of a technical investigation. The whole program will be at the expense (you will explain) of the Fogwell Institute, which has provided three research assistants. And now the staff meeting is to receive the first interim report.

Duncan Item 3. Report from Dr. Angeles, copies of which have been circulated. Any comments?

Macbeth I suggest, sir, that we invite Dr. Angeles to explain his project. Here he is . . .

Duncan Very well, Number Two. Dr. Angeles, the floor is yours.

Angeles My object, Mr. President and gentlemen, is to present our interim report in the simplest form. The facts already revealed call for immediate action. To wait for the final report would be to let the situation deteriorate. Briefly, then, I have made a preliminary study of this organization, using Batworthy's nonlinear extension of the optimal range . . .

Macbeth With internal validity checks, I hope?

Angeles Certainly. You will find a note on diagnostic procedures at Appendix K. Applying a strategy of random variables and using the Stochastic Model; applying, moreover, our experience of operations research and decision theory, we could not escape the meaningful conclusion which we have tabulated on pages 34 to 37.

Duncan Very interesting, but I really don't see . . .

Macbeth Forgive my interrupting, sir, but I think I can explain the passage which you find obscure. I was puzzled myself and asked Dr. Angeles why he rejected the simpler strategy of Filkenstein's Theorem. But he soon convinced me that quadratic programming would not, in this case, have been helpful. I think you will find the report in other respects both lucid and cogent.

Pause now and reflect, for the staff meeting has reached what is known in the bullfighting arena as the Moment of Truth. For Number One it is a question of now or never. To regain control of the situation he must at this point drop his copy of the interim report into the wastepaper basket and address Dr. Angeles in some such words as these:

Duncan All this sounds to me like gobbledygook. I haven't the least idea what you are talking about and have no reason to think that it matters. If you have any constructive comments to make on our organization, make them in plain language, stating what you think should be done. But don't talk to me as you might to a digital computer. I don't like it, don't grasp it and won't have it.

By this brusque reaction, which will reduce Dr. Angeles to twittering ineptitude, Number One can defeat the whole plot. In a moment all the vice-presidents will be admitting in chorus that the interim report is so much meaningless drivel. The founder of the Company, old Tom Tuffenuff, would have done exactly that. But today's executives are seldom men of his caliber. It takes some courage to profess a scornful ignorance among a whole group of executives, each professing to follow the whole argument. In nine cases out of ten, Number One will fail the test. He will nod his head in feigned comprehension. And once the moment has passed, he will never regain control of the meeting, which will continue on these lines:

Duncan Thank you, Mac. The report might have been worded more clearly, but I think we all understand the Doctor's point (*he looks around*).

All (*quickly*) Yes, yes. Perfectly clear.

Macbeth Well, I seem to be the dumb bunny here, but I'm still puzzled by the last half of page 41. Why should dynamic programming involve the theory of games?

Angeles I'm glad you asked that. My symbol-manipulation language is not as coherent as it should be. The page summarizes my heuristic line-balancing procedure, which leads to the nonbasic optimum solution on the next page.

Macbeth But that solution is inconsistent, surely, with the combinational analysis and topology on page 17 — look, you say here that

$$II = \frac{I}{mm} - (p + h^2)$$

What about the calculus of probabilities?

Angeles It doesn't apply to a multiperson interaction. It *would* have applied, I freely admit, had I been using a different methodology. But the conclusions would have been much the same.

Macbeth Oh, I'm not questioning that. The Zoning-Constraint would not have been affected.

Angeles Exactly! It is a question of cybernetics and a use of the minimax principle. We are basically in agreement, I think.

Macbeth   That is so. But your exhaustive algorithms leave me with a regret function which defies analysis.

Angeles (*laughing heartily*)   Good, good!

All (*smiling nervously*)   Heh, heh, heh . . .

Macbeth   Well, sir. We have, as I see it, to apply this report to the Activation of Motives in our organization. I suggest, however, that we defer action until Part II of the final report is before us, which will be in about three weeks. The matter can wait until then, I guess, but not much longer — isn't that right?

Angeles   We need a firm decision before the end of the month.

Macbeth   Right. And we shall need to discuss Part II at some length before we outline our program.

Duncan (*apprehensively*)   At some length?

Macbeth   Well, we need to know what we are doing.

Duncan (*crushed*)   I suppose so . . .

Macbeth   And I feel we should thank Dr. Angeles for all his help.

All   Yes, yes. Very valuable indeed.

Angeles   I could never have produced this Interim Report without the help of the three research assistants provided for me by the Fogwell Institute. Miss Weard and her two sisters have done a fine job. Might I convey to them the President's thanks?

Duncan   I suppose so.

Angeles   They will greatly appreciate it.

Duncan   And now, Dr. Angeles, you will be wanting to get back to your investigations. Thank you, Doctor . . . Now — Item 4. The estimate for repairing the power-house roof. Mr. Macduff?

Number One will bluster over Item 4 but he has nevertheless lost ground. By next week he will have to face another discussion with Dr. Angeles and still without the least idea of what is to be discussed. Then will come the final report. In this Dr. Angeles will include his masterpiece, the model to illustrate the Head Office Social System. As this represents the last deadly stroke, it is worth reproducing in full. Here it is:

At the sight of this diagram, Number One will utter a hollow groan. "Oh, *no!*" he will whisper, "not *that!*" But *that* is nevertheless what he has to face. All he can do is to retire to bed with a migraine, leaving Number Two to carry out the planned reorganization. Whenever Number One shows signs of recovery, a mere flourish of the diagram (Plate 1), a mere distant echo of Dr. Angeles' voice, will be enough to bring on a relapse. The time for Number One's retirement is near and there can be no doubt as to who his successor must be. Nor is there any doubt as to what you do with Dr. Angeles as soon as the farewells have been said. "Out!" you will say briefly, proving once more that the hired assassin becomes unwelcome after the deed has been done. Do you hesitate to use this method of removing Number One? Do you recoil from treating any man with such calculated cruelty? If so, the feeling does you credit. You have a loftier moral code and higher ethical principles than many a minister of religion. You have all the selfless motivation which may fit you for the second post in any organization; and there, as Number Two, you are likely to remain. For the Number Ones of this world are ultimately ruthless. They will use any means to gain their end, and if Management Science looks usefully lethal, that is the weapon they will use. Shrink from this nebulous dagger and you will soon be thinking (and quite rightly, from your point of view) that to be Number One is hardly worth the pain and effort. One day, by your fireside, with pipe lit and coffee at your elbow, you will say to your wife, "Ambition is all very well . . . but I have come to like being Number Two. Do you know, I sometimes begin to suspect that I shall never be anything else?" And your wife, to whom the same suspicion has been a certainty for the last six years, will calmly and smilingly agree.

11. THE PARKINSEY REPORT

AN INDUSTRIAL empire such as you aspire to rule is not a mechanical structure in which steel girders rest on concrete blocks. It is rather the result of a biological process in which seed and mating, growth and fertility play the dominant role. The world of business is an avenue in which parasites cling to the trees; a garden where weeds spring up among the flowers; an orchard in which bees carry the pollen of managerial science from one plant to another; a wood in which the branches of economic theory are strictly for the birds. In this wonderland of nature the facts of life are not to be ignored. One such fact is sex and we should be wrong to pretend otherwise. Victorian authors who dealt with the business world were reticent about the sexual aspects although all too prone to smiles of furtive innuendo. Today we have learned to discuss these matters frankly and openly, giving our children illustrated pamphlets about the flowers and the bees and telling each other (perhaps too often) that the mysteries of nature are really very beautiful. We can no longer disguise the fact that the Corporation has Sex.

Like any flower or shrub, the industrial plant is either male or female. There is not, however, the external sex difference observable in the animal world. Sex determination in business is more a matter for the expert. Your success in life may depend, however, on your becoming such an expert. Before joining a Company as vice-president or president you must discover its sex. Nor is this quite as difficult as some authors have chosen to pretend. After all, sex characteristics in a Company are broadly similar to those found in a human being. Do not so oversimplify the problem, however, as to identify the corporate sexes as Sale and Resale. While there may be a male tendency in wholesale business and a female bias in the retail, it would be quite wrong to think that this is invariable. Such a crude analysis would leave the sex undetermined in many an enterprise while causing misunderstanding and subsequent embarrassment as a result of mistaking the sex of others. No mistakes need be made by the observer who knows what the sex characteristics are.

A male corporation is to be identified, first of all, by its rough exterior. It may be fairly tidy but it has made no effort to look attractive. The layout is more practical than pleasing, the machinery unconcealed and the paint-work conservative and drab. Combined with this rugged appearance is an assertiveness in advertising, a rather crude claim to offer what is at once the cheapest and the best. The organization is extrovert, outgoing and inquisitive, its representatives more likely to visit another organization than wait to be visited. With this type of company's boastful manner goes a carelessness over details, a failure to check the outgoing mail, a neglect to clean the windows, an omission to test the fire appliance. Added to all this is the male extravagance. Faced with a decline in gross turnover, the male urge is not so much to economize as to seek some other source of income. It has been suggested that the male corporation is polygamous, showing a tendency to form temporary attachments or engage at least in casual flirtations. This theory cannot be accepted without certain reservations but that it has some basis is undeniable. While many or perhaps most male organizations are loyal to their chief business associate, others have a roving tendency and all (it may be) a roving eye. Last of all, the male corporation is apt to treat its male offspring with some severity, telling them to fight their own battles and punishing any whose gambling losses seem excessive.

The female corporation shows all the opposite characteristics. Its factory buildings are prettily sited and smartly kept, with pastel shades in the paintwork and flower beds near the gate. But with the attractive layout there goes a certain modesty. Some parts of the production process are usually concealed and there may be a certain reticence shown in other ways — as affecting past associations, for example, and even the age of the plant. In the female organization there can be too much fuss over details, an insistence on exact procedure and an overemphasis on the appearance (as opposed to the reality) of competence. In general policy the female trend is towards economy and financial caution. Faced with a recession, the female corporation hastens to curtail expenditure and reduce the dividend. In general negotiations this type of company is more introvert, less outgoing. It will receive representatives of another firm but is unlikely to return the visit. There is, last of all, a difference in its attitude towards the young. In a female corporation the maternal instinct is highly developed. Towards its offspring there is a protective attitude, a lenience which often goes beyond the bounds of its generally conservative finance.

The sex life of the Corporation has been made the sub-

ject of a monumental work, *The Parkinsey Report* (in two
volumes), which it would be impossible even to summarize
in such a chapter as this. To those volumes the reader may

turn for a full account of corporate reproduction, with
chapters on Merger, on premergital relationships, abnor-
malities and divorce. For the present purpose it should

suffice to note that Mergers occur and that the rising executive should never lose sight of the fact. When a Merger
takes place the advantage lies normally with the male
corporation, which has been acquisitive and active. It is to
such a corporation that the rising executive should attach
himself, remembering that the reorganization which ac-
companies the Merger will create opportunities for those
who look ahead. Executives on the female side are more
likely to be displaced and thrust aside. For them the future
is indeed pregnant with trouble and they have only themselves to blame. Through ignorance of the facts of life,
they have found themselves on the wrong side of the
Merger. Theirs is a fate which others should seek to avoid.
Always be on the male or active side. And when you come
to hold high office, maintain at all costs the masculine
character of your firm. Merge but never submerge.

But Merger in its conventional and accustomed form is
not the only hazard in corporate sex relationships. Behind
the whole Victorian attitude towards sex lay the fears
of elopement. The romantic character of this practice
is well established in fiction. We all know the procedure — the bribed maidservant, the love letter, the girl
at the window, the young man in the moonlight, the
assignation in the churchyard, the ladder, the flight, the
pursuit, the marriage. What the Victorians feared, however, was not so much the runaway match as the sordid
betrayal. Sequel to the real elopement was the demand
for money. For a substantial sum the blackmailer would
return the girl unharmed and unmarried. For an even
larger sum the blackmailer would agree to marry the girl
he had already seduced. In either event the victim's family

was involved in anxiety, discredit and expense; thus pro-
viding an example which other families would be all the
more eager to avoid. Similar to this bugbear of an earlier
generation, less familiar today, is the Takeover Bid of the
twentieth century. As among corporations, the Takeover
Bid is the equivalent of the Elopement or Seduction. In
more conservative business circles it is looked upon with a
mixture of fascination and horror, disapproval and envy.

   In Britain more especially the Takeover Bid (as contrasted with the ordinary merger) began to make news
as from about 1951. The wartime weight of taxation which
peacetime extravagance tended if anything to increase, had
lessened the shareholder's interest in a taxable dividend.
Company tax (56 per cent in 1952 as compared with 37

per cent in 1938) discouraged companies from admitting to a profit. Bored with working for nothing or interested only in capital gains, directors took little interest in certain developments which were to affect the value of their stock. Consumer demands were changing and shifting, heavier industries being displaced by light. Companies under conservative management failed to adjust themselves to the market situation, having adjusted themselves all too well in respect of the tax. They amassed liquid assets, paid low dividends, undervalued their real estate, allowed for depreciation where there was none and saw their stock quoted at a price which only the small dividend could justify. Companies in this position are vulnerable.

From an earlier analysis of sex differentiation in companies (see page 201) it will be obvious to the reader that these companies are predominantly female. Of those affected by Takeover Bids in 1951-61 the majority, in fact, were in retail distribution, or real estate. The battles took place in and around hotels and multiple stores, the missiles used being suits and socks and sausages, bakeries, bedding and beer.

The battles which raged from Claridge's to the Savoy in 1953-58 were, however, exceptional. The normal takeover involves no rival bidder but concerns only the Wolfson and his prey. What are the commercial equivalents of the assignation, the ladder and the race for Gretna Green? These are best illustrated in a form in which weeks of negotiation can be conveniently compressed into minutes. The scene, let us suppose, is the boardroom of Doolittle & Hording, the company which controls a chain of 250 grocery stores. The portraits of Doolittle and Hording look down with approval on their sons-in-law, Dooless and Hordmore, the Company's Chairman, respectively, and Treasurer. The other directors present are Hidewell, Fusty and Lacking. The room is decorated in lilac and silver with chilly daffodils on light oak and a slightly feminine taste in curtains. The company is long established, female, conservative and undervalued. In one corner is a bronze statue of Constipation by Rodin. As the curtain rises we find the directors in a state of twittering panic, with the chairman on the phone.

Chairman (*into receiver*)   Yes, I see . . . Quite . . . I realize that . . . But you feel reasonably sure? . . . Thanks, Dick. Goodbye. (*To the others*) Yes, our guess was correct. Mayfair Investments *were* buying our shares for Isaac Cottonwolf and the Mail Order Group. They probably hold 12 per cent of our equity.

Hordmore   With the 20 per cent we hold, this board can defy him.

Lacking   But he is still buying. The shares had risen again by eleven this morning.

Hidewell   Why should he pick on *us?*

Fusty   What harm have we ever done?

Chairman   He wants our cash and our freeholds at a bargain price. And our shareholders (if they fall for it) will receive voteless "A" shares in Mail Order. Oh, dear, what will become of us? (*Enter typist with note for the chairman*) And now Cottonwolf is believed to own 16 per cent! There is nothing else for it. We shall have to raise the dividend.

Directors (*incredulous*)   *Raise the dividend??*

Hordmore   Unthinkable!

Lacking   But I don't see *why?*

Chairman   You don't see anything. We must declare an interim dividend of 8 per cent.

Hordmore   But that would make *15 per cent* for the year! What about our reserves? What about our depreciation account?

Chairman   It is a hard decision but we have no alternative. Agreed?

All (*reluctantly*)   Suppose so . . .

Chairman (*telephoning*)   Tell the shareholders that we are paying an interim dividend of eight per cent. Add that our prospects are terrific! (*To the others*) That should do the trick! (*Telephone rings*) Yes, Dooless here. What? *What's* that? . . . Oh, thanks. (*To the others*) The shareholders don't believe that we shall pay as good a dividend after Cottonwolf has withdrawn. He now holds 19 per cent of the equity!

Hordmore   But of *course* we shan't pay 15 per cent after the crisis is over! I hope that is understood?

Chairman   It is understood by the shareholders all right . . . (*Telephone rings*) Good heavens! . . . Yes, Mr. Cottonwolf . . . You are making a formal offer? . . . How much? . . . Fifty-two shillings? . . . Do I accept? Nonsense. I must put your proposal to the Board . . . (*To the others*) Do we accept? (*They all shake their heads*) No, we do *not* accept. We defy you! What is more, sir, we feel sure that the shareholders will take our advice and refuse to sell! (*Rings off. Makes a call*) Tell the shareholders that the Board advises them not to sell. (*Rings off*)

Hordmore   Remember, Dooless, that we hold 20 per cent of the shares between us. He cannot gain the 90 per cent he needs to make the rest sell, and his offer is conditional on that; or so I assume.

Chairman   It *is* conditional, as you say. And many of the shareholders will support us.

Fusty   But how many?

Chairman (*into receiver*)   How many of the shareholders have agreed to accept Mr. Cottonwolf's offer? . . . I see . . . How many have rejected it? . . . I see. Thank you. (*To the others*) He now controls 43 per cent of the shares, and we only 31 per cent. All we can do is offer a still higher dividend. Shall we do that?

All (*gloomily*)   Might as well.

Chairman (*into receiver*)   Tell the shareholders that we are raising the interim dividend to 12 per cent . . . What's that? No? Good God! (*To the others*) He has 47 per cent of the shares. Let's see what effect our dividend has.

Hidewell   I don't see that it will have any.

Fusty   I think it may backfire.

Lacking   But why? The shareholders ought to be impressed. (*Clerk enters with evening paper, which he lays before the chairman*) What's this?

Chairman   Good heavens! Cottonwolf says that shareholders will still receive the increased dividend even after he gains control. That is bound to influence them! Oh, dear! (*Into receiver*) How many shares do we control now? . . . Is that all? And Cottonwolf? No! Really? Well, thanks for telling me. (*To the rest*) He holds 51 per cent and he has made his offer unconditional!

Hordmore (*groaning*)   He controls the Company!

Fusty (*wailing*)   He can replace the Board!

Hidewell (*sighing*)   He can sell our freeholds and take the shops on a lease!

Lacking   Ah, but we can write to the *Times!* Yes, and we can ask for a Board of Trade Investigation!

Chairman   Don't deceive yourself, Lacking. We have been defeated. We must surrender and make the best terms we can.

The Takeover Bid does not lead, of necessity, to an un-happy merger. The fact must be faced, however, that the bidder is usually polygamous. He has a harem, with wives, concubines, children and grandchildren. This is called a Group and is remarkable these days for the variety of its interests. Mergers of the traditional pattern were between firms in roughly the same line of business. They involved either the elimination of rivals or an integration of the whole process, as when a manufacturer sought to control both his raw materials and his retail outlets. But modern commercial empires are often as incongruous as they are vast, owing more of their success to the offspring's initiative than to the parent's control. But they depend too much, nevertheless, upon a single man; upon one who is liable, like any other, to illness, accident and age. Nor can a sequence of supermen be maintained forever, or even perhaps for long. The Board of Directors, having been trampled upon by one tyrant, are seldom in the mood to seek another. They may prefer a change and a rest. This is the moment for which you, the organization man, have been waiting. You are the man chosen to fill the presidential chair. At long last you have reached the summit. Henceforward, you are Number One.

You are President of the Corporation. Whether you possess all the essential qualifications for the office may be doubtful. But one quality you must clearly have demonstrated is the ability to distinguish between the sexes. In each of the mergers you will have contrived to be on the male side. In planning your career you must have consistently chosen the male or active role, each merger thus proving to your advantage. It is partly to your prescience in this respect that you will owe your ultimate achievement, your appointment as president of a group.

Remember, however, that sex in industry is not immutable. However manly your corporation may be, it can lose its male characteristics. It may become financially cautious, reserved and prim, with swollen deposits and a too well rounded personality. With dividends restricted and waste reduced, with strait-laced advertising and impressive statistics, the public image may totally change. While abreast of the times, it may become vulnerable and diffident, prettily appealing and weak. Then it is that the day of reckoning may come. There will be a disquieting rumor in Wall Street and your stock will begin to rise. You will realize, with horror, that there has been a change of sex,

that the Takeover Group may itself be taken over and that what has happened in the past to others may happen in the end to you.

Osborn

12. THE THIRD LAW

LET US ASSUME in this last chapter that you, the reader of this page, have gained one of the highest positions in the modern world. With the help of this book (thumbed and dog-eared beneath the pillow) you have gone from strength to strength, surviving conflicts and mergers so as to become finally the president of the Stupendic Gigantsome Metal Corporation, which has a capital of one billion billion and an industrial empire deployed from Alaska to Peru. There are only five other comparable posts in the world and each of them filled by a Rockefeller or Rothschild. You have a colossal salary and an even larger expense account. You hold an option to buy stock, when you retire, on staggeringly favorable terms. To your fourth and most glamorous wife you complain on occasion of overwork, referring obliquely to the burden of responsibility you have been called upon to bear. Your sigh is accompanied, however, by a look of pity for all who have failed to gain a like eminence.

As in other monarchies, you must be alert for signs of revolt. It is told of more than one legendary king that he would disguise himself and mingle with the crowd in the market place, listening to careless chatter and assessing the public reaction to his latest decree. Were you to do the same, wandering unnoticed through saloon, club and congressional lobby, you would overhear the murmurings of sedition. There are people, you would gather, who think that Stupendic is too powerful for the public good. If there *has* to be any such concentration of wealth, you might hear it said, then it should be vested in the state and made subject to democratic control. Nationalization, you would note, is some people's answer to monopoly. The criticism you would hear on all sides is that Stupendic does not do enough for the public welfare. It exists to make a profit for its stockholders and still more for its directors. It takes too much and contributes too little. It is a soulless machine doing nothing for the nation as a whole. Back in your modest penthouse on the roof of the Walledoff Stupendia, you will think bitterly of man's ingratitude.

There is little you can learn from ingratitude as such but folly points inversely to the truth. And it is the cry for nationalization that should draw your attention to the Stupendic's chief merit. For the Stupendic Gigantsome

has the advantage — whatever its other faults — of being supernational. It is among the forces which work blindly for improved relationships as between one country and another. This is a matter not of deliberate policy but of habitual outlook; the outlook of men whose business is worldwide. The model for supernational affairs is not to be found so much at Geneva or The Hague as in the board-room of an oil corporation. To nationalize such an under-taking, making it the mere instrument of government, is to drag it down to the politician's parochial level. The larger corporations are not among the groups which clamor against war; and this is extremely fortunate, for conflict widens (as we all realize) in direct proportion to the de-mand for peace. But they do represent the international outlook as found among scientists, bankers, and circus clowns. They are thus in several respects a power for good, having long since solved the sort of problem which the world's foreign ministers are still struggling to define.

But while the remedy urged by fools is obviously worse than the disease, the feeling may linger that the disease is there. Among your colleagues you will note a trace of anxiety, an eagerness to justify themselves, an urge to liberalize the Corporation's policy. The period of ruthless competition has passed. The battle for supremacy is over. With prosperity assured, the time has come for high-minded patronage and public spirit. It is the Corporation's aim to serve the people or, better still, to serve mankind. One aspect of this growing liberality is represented by the professionalism of management. The manager of today adds to his professional training an atmosphere of profes-sional etiquette. "Is this good business?" may be his first question, and "What is the tax angle?" his second, but "Is it ethical?" is now his third. In times past the loftiest references to "service" were the invariable preliminary to someone being swindled. This, however, is no longer true. The ethics are often as ethical, or very nearly as ethical, as they sound. The businessman takes his place alongside the judge, the preacher and the surgeon, being prevented by his cloth from doing this or that. To buy at the lowest price and sell at the highest is no longer the object in view. He asks only to serve the public to the best of his ability, showing a helpful benevolence towards his trade rivals (now few and unimportant), a generous paternalism towards the prime producers, a candid integrity towards the buying public. He is among the latest aspirants to pro-fessional status, full of management jargon to prove his special knowledge, full of Rotary Club idealism to prove his essential worth. The directors of Stupendic Gigant-some are among the most ethical of these very ethical men. The Stupendic contribution to many a Cause has left the charitable organization prostrate, its officials unemployed and aimless. There is a scale of generosity that can practically kill.

Foremost among the Stupendic liberals is Walter Wilcox, whose niggardly private expenditure is nicely balanced by his lavish attitude towards money that is not his. Patient research has now established an interesting correlation between these apparently contrasting attitudes, showing that public extravagance and private meanness are nearly always found in close association. Wilcox himself provided a good example of this when subletting his apartment to Frank Fairfield. It so happened that Wilcox's vacation coincided with Frank's period for repair and redecoration. At something above the proper rent Frank's family had shelter until the builders had gone and Frank thought no more of the matter until after Wilcox's return. He then had a telephone call to which he replied as follows:

Fairfield That you, Walter? Had a good vacation?

Wilcox Yes, thanks. I attended the Summer School at Pennsylvania State College as guest speaker on personnel management. Most enjoyable, with all expenses paid.

Fairfield That's fine. And I hope you found the apartment in order?

Wilcox Well, Frank, that is what I want to talk to you about. First of all, I left some supplies in the kitchen, which I see you have used. I made a note at the time and it reads like this: half a pound of butter, two eggs, four segments of cheese, a rasher of bacon and an opened can of beans; also, a half bottle, half empty, of brandy, and a whole bottle, two-thirds full, of cooking sherry. I hope you will agree that my list is correct?

Fairfield   I suppose so. Can't say I noticed.

Wilcox   No? You mayn't have noticed in that case that you left some apples behind and four bottles of beer?

Fairfield   Oh, did I? Well keep them.

Wilcox   Unfortunately, I don't drink beer. And the apples are going rotten. So I have been trying to work out a valuation. I have just replaced the brandy, which is kept for medicinal purposes, so I know the cost of that. The exact price of the cooking sherry I don't recall but will ask the grocer. Now, as regards the butter . . .

Fairfield   For heaven's sake! I'll give you five dollars and call it quits.

Wilcox   I wanted to make sure that you agreed with me in principle . . .

Fairfield   Yes, yes, yes. Stop pestering me and I'll agree to anything.

Wilcox   Thank you. I do appreciate that. You can rely upon my integrity.

Fairfield   Yes, yes. Goodbye! (*Rings off*)

At the Board Meeting that afternoon the question comes up of the Corporation's contribution to the Family Planning Clinic. Last year's donation came to $10,000 and the proposal from the Treasurer was to keep it at that figure. The Clinic is fulfilling a social need but can receive no

public funds because of the Catholic vote. On the whole, says the Treasurer, $10,000 would seem to be about right, more than the contribution made last year by Dithering and Littleworth but less than the contribution from Splendley Checkwright, Inc. Would the Board agree to $10,000?

Chairman   Is the Treasurer's motion seconded?

Fairfield   I second that.

Chairman   Is the motion agreed?

Wilcox   One moment, Mr. Chairman. I move, as an amendment that we increase our subscription to $25,000. It does not do, in a matter like this, to worry too much about —

Chairman   One moment, please. Is Mr. Wilcox's amendment seconded?

Wadsworth   Yes, I second that. (He *would!*)

Chairman (hopeless)   Very well then. Wilcox?

Wilcox   Well, Mr. Chairman, I do feel that a larger amount would be fully justified. The Clinic is doing splendid work and not merely in family limitation. In close association with Dr. Dripfast is a team of research workers from Philadelphia. These are trying to investigate the economic and educational level of families in which the children number more than six. The report they hope to prepare should be of the greatest value. Nor should we underestimate the social value of the Clinic's general influence. On this subject more than one point of view is possible. That I fully recognize. No fair-minded man can well ignore the religious objections that have been voiced against family planning. Having listened to many a discussion on this subject I feel that, on balance, the case for supporting this clinic is a very strong one. That being so, I feel that we should be not merely fair, but generous. I have no patience, I confess, with doubts as to whether we can afford a larger amount. After all, taking into consideration the scale of our finances, another ten or fifteen thousand dollars represents an almost negligible sum. Let's not be mean over this. Let's be open-handed for once! If we are ever to be liberal, this is the time!

We need not record the whole of the debate, which lasts an hour and three quarters and ends with a subscription of $12,500, but the scene is incomplete without a brief extract from the private conversation which ensued between Fairfield and Wilcox.

Wilcox Just a word with you Frank, about the matter we discussed over the telephone.

Fairfield (resigned) Yes?

Wilcox It has occurred to me since that I can't claim on those beer bottles. You know how it is — the rumors that would get about.

Fairfield Look, Walter. Here is ten dollars in cash. Will you take it and close the subject?

Wilcox (shocked) You don't understand. It is not the *money* I am worrying about but the *principle*. By my reckoning you owe me $3.35 — allowing the apples to be worth about as much as the cheese and bacon. This is not strictly true, but I want to be fair. The question is, how to dispose of the beer.

Fairfield   In the trashcan.

Wilcox   That would be unfair to you. No, I can't agree to that. How would it be if I made the bottles up into a parcel and brought them to the office, where you could collect them?

Fairfield   All right. Do that. Here is a five-dollar bill. Take $3.35 out of it.

Wilcox   Sorry, I don't have the change.

Fairfield   Give the balance to the Clinic.

Wilcox   Very generous of you. You shall have the receipt. I hope, by the way, there are no hard feelings about this Family Planning Cause? I realize that you are not very keen about it. But even another $2500 makes a difference. The Cause, as I think, deserves the time we gave to it.

Fairfield   We'll hope so. Tell me, Walter, what was the amount of your own subscription?

Wilcox   I gave them ten dollars and promised to use my influence. What about you?

Fairfield   I gave them fifty dollars and told them to go to hell!

The point is that Wilcox, being privately mean and niggling, finds compensation in being generous with the Company's money. Fairfield, being careful with the Company's money, finds compensation in being careless with his own. This correlation is known to be normal.

Urged on by Walter Wilcox and his kind, the Stupendic Gigantsome has, you will find, an extremely liberal outlook. It is a good influence, farsighted and generous. It is internationally minded and is guilty of none of the crimes of which it is accused. It is far more efficient than it would be if nationalized. All this will be obvious to you, as president. What will also be obvious is that the Corporation is too big. On the one hand, the process of integration, rationalization and absorption which brought the Stupendic into existence must seem inevitable in retrospect (and probably was). On the other hand, the result is something too complex to survive. Like the reconstructed dinosaurs illustrated in books of prehistory, the Stupendic has become too cumbersome to adjust itself to change. It will come to be described, in Kipling's words, as a pachydermatous anachronism. Nor is it obvious what anyone can do about it.

The complexity of the Stupendic Gigantsome is apparent from its organization chart, its hierarchy, its rigidity, its uniformity. And what people fail to realize is that the complexities do not stem from policy but merely from size. Given the mere numbers and distances involved, the complex organization becomes inevitable. Decisions become impersonal and distant, attributable not to a person but to "Them." It may be the Board's action but on whose advice? With complexity comes the need for rules and precedents. With it comes the tide of paperwork, the statistics and returns. With it, finally, comes the effort to be alike. There are people, it is true, who have taken fright about the organization man. There are corporations who would like to reverse the trend. But this uniformity comes not from fashion but from the nature of things. If personnel are to be interchangeable, they *must* be alike. They must be prefabricated to a standard pattern. How else can the system work? The pattern is complicated enough as it is. To introduce the variables associated with personality would make is impossible. In light fiction it is assumed that a retired British Colonel must conform to an accepted pattern (Dammit! What?) just as Generals must be choleric and professors absent-minded. Part of the old army officer's usefulness lay in the fact that commanders could be replaced without any perceptible change in outlook, discipline or routine. So it is with the executive sent to Honolulu by the Intercontinental Oil Company. Arriving as successor in oilsmanship to someone whose training is identical, he carries on smoothly from the point where his predecessor left off. The replacement of one peppery and whiskered Colonel by another, the succession of one "oil-minded" executive by the next, these are the sort of changes observable in the Palace forecourt where the sentries may be relieved but the colorful ritual remains the same.

Most of the Giant Corporation's complexity is the result of size. But some of its complexity is the result of age. Few of the big companies are still under their founder's presidency. It might be true to say that the founder was the grandfather, on an average, or contemporary with the grandfathers, of the present directors. By this stage one of two things must happen. Either a grandson of the founder is president, with a dynastic title like Rothsfeller III or else the management has passed into the hands of the experts. In either event the initial momentum will have been lost.

Rothsfeller III lacks, as a rule, the ruthless virility of Rothsfeller I. He lacks the original propellant — the urge to
escape from poverty. He offers, instead, the picture of
authority, dignity, culture and charm. For governing an
established empire — one he could never have acquired —
the third in line can be very well fitted indeed. But what
about the fourth? As in all monarchies, the moment comes
when the successor to the throne is a weakling, an intellectual, a sportsman or aesthete. Control passes inevitably
to the experts, the efficiency men, the figureheads of the
managerial revolution.

A figurehead, in this modern sense, is a head full of
figures. You have risen to high office by application,
knowledge, loyalty, marriage, foresight, hardness, persist-
ence and luck. The one quality you have never had and
never wanted is the quality of leadership. Some of your
rivals had it and were long since discarded as insubordinate.
Men in the smaller companies have it, but what can they
do when brought into competition with the Stupendic
Gigantsome? For running the organization you have all
that is needed: ability, health, versatility and ruthlessness.
You have no touch of genius, nor is it required. But leadership is essential if the Corporation is to survive for long; and
leadership is what you lack. How could it be otherwise?
Given that quality, you could never have risen by the only
route that was open to you. So far as the Stupendic
Gigantsome is concerned, leadership is not on the menu.
Enormous as the assets may be, leadership is not one of
them.

What is leadership? It is the art of so indicating a distant goal as to make all else seem trivial. When the natural
leader has finished describing the Holy Grail, the Eternal

City, the Glory of France or the Honor of the Regiment, all immediate privations and perils are thought irrelevant. It was with something of the same fervor that old Ben Bandersnatch (the real founder of Stupendic) called his men about him on the eve of the first great merger. "Boys," he said, "we must think big. If this deal goes through, we shall control a quarter of the industry!" Who, in the light of his enthusiasm, could have asked for a salary raise? Who on the assembly floor could have begun discussing a thirty-hour week? Who complained, for that matter, if kept at the office all night? It was reward sufficient to come home, white and haggard, vowing your wife to secrecy. "Don't tell anyone, Susan, but old Ben is on the warpath. I think he's brought it off. The news should be all over the world on Thursday. Gee, I'm worn out!" Assume, if you like, that Susan's husband had nothing to do with the deal. Suspect, if you will, that he was not even wanted at the office. The fact remains that he was living in the presence of a drama beside which his own affairs could be forgotten. This was the mood in which men fought at Austerlitz, Trafalgar or the Normandy Beachhead. It is under an inspired leader that the soldier comes to regard his own possible death as a mere incident. It is under an industrial leader that the workman can grudge his own wage as a debit figure in the firm's tottering finances. At least in the early and adventurous phase of an industry, the excitement can mean more to people than the pay. "In those days," they can boast afterwards, "men were *Men*." But this is not the situation with which *you* have to deal. The old hazardous days you never even knew.

What confronts you and the other experts is not adventure but decay. Decadence is something, therefore, which

you need to understand. You may associate decadence in
your mind with black satin pajamas and absinthe, remark-
ing (and correctly) that your head office is comparatively
free from both. But that is to misunderstand the nature of
decay. When a tree decays it is not normally from sickness
and never (one assumes) from sin. It decays because it has
reached its maximum growth, maintaining that size and
weight for the period usual with that type of tree. It cannot live forever in any case. Institutions, whether political
or industrial, are not essentially different. For them too,
maturity leads to decay. But human beings differ from
trees in that they know what is happening. For them the
chief symptom of decadence is the knowledge of how little
time is left. Youth, by contrast, is the knowledge of how
long is still to go. This awareness of the future is not entirely conscious, being manifest more from what people do
than from what they say. It is apparent, above all, from
how long things are meant to last. In most modern work-
manship the foreknowledge of impermanence is clearly
there. The artist has taken as much trouble as the circumstances would seem to justify. And this, surely, is the
essential character of decadence.

So it is with Stupendic Gigantsome. Its growth is finished. It could, in theory, absorb its chief rival in a final
merger. This, however, is prevented by law. Nor would
it seem advisable even as a matter of policy. The better
plan is to preserve the appearance of competition while dis-
creetly agreeing on prices, wages and quality. So the
Stupendic Gigantsome will retain its present share of the
trade, expanding one branch and curtailing another, introducing automation where practicable and changing the
angle of its advertising policy from time to time. It would

seem to be one of the more permanent features of the industrial landscape. Its decay, nevertheless, has begun, its progress showing more dignity than vigor.

But why *should* Stupendic collapse? It will fall a victim to Parkinson's Third Law, which is this: *Expansion means complexity and complexity, decay;* or, to put it even more plainly — The more complex, the sooner dead. Decay, eventually, is inevitable, for no institution can last forever. But the process of decline and fall can be retarded, at least, by any chief executive who knows what is taking place. You must be alert for the signs of woodworm and dryrot, fungus and rust. You must hear the deathwatch beetle's stealthy approach. Are there too many on the Board of Directors? Are the initials too numerous on each invoice and bill? Is everyone nowadays too specialized and secretive? Is there too wide a distribution of documents and memoranda? Is the prevailing complacence enough to suffocate? Is the hearse actually at the door?

To measure the deathwatch beetle's advance, you should begin by looking afresh at the buildings. First, there is the original shed of 1912 in which the enterprise began, now a museum. Next there is the factory building of 1925, vast, sprawling, and impatiently thrown together; a mere roof over the machines. Then you have the Head Office of 1934, built after the great merger and replete with marble and bronze, wrought iron and oak. Across the highway are the frantic extensions of 1944, fulfilling the purpose of all temporary buildings, which is to occupy for fifty years a site that is wanted for something else. Finally, there is the latest structure, built in 1960 to house the newer departments: Public Relations, Personnel Management, Cultural Activities, Welfare and Guidance, Recreation and Sport.

It is built on a frame of light alloy and constructed of compressed wood, fiberglass, polyethylene and paper. What the
visitor takes to be the result of a burst pipe is the Japanese
Garden. What look like chalkmarks on the walls are the
murals by Sakuma Musashi. The premises are notable not
only for their lightweight structure but for their wood-
wool insulation and freely circulating hot air. Designed by
Professor Schnitzelbaum of the Michigan University
School of Architecture, they represent the latest trends in
structure and outlook. What is manifest about them is that
they will not last for long and that they are unrelated to the
factory's purpose. Whether the Stupendic Group will
flourish for another twenty years may still be an open
question but the builders of its latest extension did not give
it more than a decade. If structures such as these tell a story,
it is of directors ending their service and parasites ready to
quit. Decay, if not yet apparent, is certainly expected.

Having looked at the buildings, send for the salaries list
and see what value the Corporation sets on enterprise.
Executives are broadly of two kinds, those technically capable of starting something new and those merely able to
administer the organization that exists. Which is the more
important — a new product or a smooth procedure? There
is usually some lip-service to innovation and progress but
the real scale of values is expressed in the salary checks.
Who matters more, the engineer or the accountant, the
chemist or the clerk? Did the executive vice-president gain
office by discovering the possibilities of a by-product or by
running B Division without friction? Both types of ability
may be valued but which is valued more? Where the highest value is placed on routine competence, the process of
decay has begun.

Last of these preliminaries, visit the most remote outpost of the Stupendic Empire, the experimental farm in Alaska or the research unit in Peru. Discover what the scientists are doing and then ask them the crucial question: When were you last visited by a director of the firm? If the answer is "Last year" the situation is bad. If the answer is "In 1958" the situation is worse. If the answer is "Never" the situation is almost beyond remedy. For while decay at the center may take the form of fussy interference, this is consistent with a neglect of things more distant. The running down of the central machine will be manifest first in the peripheral areas, the places to which central authority can barely extend. It is at the furthest of these — on the Hadrian's Wall, as it were, of a declining empire — that the breakdown is most obvious. That the cohorts are understrength is less significant than the fact that no one has come to inspect them. The Empire may still exist but its energy is dwindling and will presently vanish. Where this is happening the process of decay is well advanced.

What is the remedy? In theory the best plan would be to reverse the whole centralizing trend, restoring a measure of independence to the units which have been absorbed. There are instances of this being done with good results. But there are situations in which the same remedy might not apply. Were it feasible, would it be effective? Were it effective, could it be done? Assuming that these doubts must arise and cannot be dispelled, and assuming therefore that size and complexity have come to stay, there is no cure for decadence. The Stupendic will eventually have to face the competition of people who work instead of argue, of people to whom progress means more than just a longer weekend. For the basic disease there is no remedy.

Something can be done, however, to retard its conquest, and it lies with you, as president, to point the way.

What is the policy to be? The situation is one which might be compared, superficially, with that faced by a hotel proprietor who has returned, after a long absence, to find the hotel neglected. The rooms are dirty and the paintwork has suffered, the service is bad and the food is worse. Servants who are perfectly capable of good work have picked up idle and slovenly habits. There are several possible remedies but the quickest and most effective is to announce a cocktail party for two hundred guests, to be followed (after three days) by a Banquet and (two days later) by a Ball. Cooks, waiters and barmen suddenly find themselves faced by a major crisis, with problems as numerous as they seem insoluble. Their morale rises overnight and the hotel becomes a different place. Any other organization can be at least temporarily revived in the same way. The technique is to announce a new program in three phases. Phase I is well within the staff's known capacity. Phase II is extremely difficult, and Phase III apparently impossible. Faced with tasks of this order and in this sequence, any organization must pull itself together.

But no organization can last forever. Even while the Stupendic executives are rallying for their last great effort, and even while you, their president, are trying to display all the gifts of leadership you do not really possess, another and a younger man has his foot in the door of another and more virile organization. His career has just begun, his present desk being his first. He is unmarried and has no apartment, almost seeming to live at the office. He refers only indirectly to his education at Exeter and Yale and he barely mentions the gains and losses which result from his

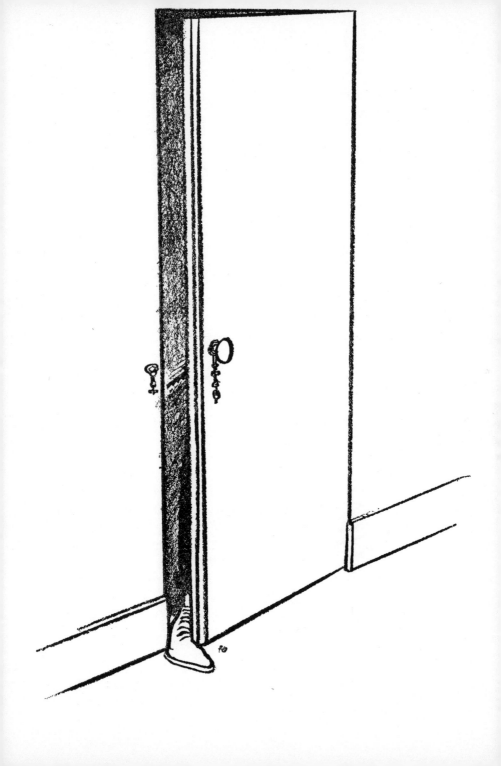

playing the market. His firm, as compared with Stupendic, is in a new and promising field of industrial enterprise — one pretty certain to expand. He is not too solemn about his work, preferring levity to gravity. The future lies no longer with you but with him. He will rise, as you did, to the top.

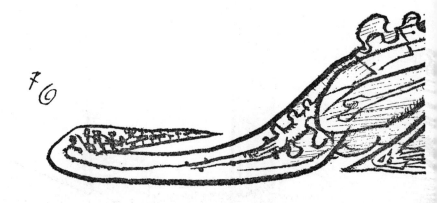